Announcing the Monster

Shah Alam Khan

AAKAR

Announcing the Monster
Shah Alam Khan

First Published 2019

ISBN 978-93-5002-616-8

Published by
AAKAR BOOKS
28 E Pocket IV, Mayur Vihar Phase I
Delhi 110 091 India
aakarbooks@gmail.com

Laser Typeset at
Arpit Printographers, Delhi

Printed at
Sapra Brothers, Noida

Dedicated to the loving memory of
Islam Khan,
who like me, was wary of monsters

The worst illiterate is the political illiterate, he doesn't hear, doesn't speak, nor participates in the political events. He doesn't know the cost of life, the price of the bean, of the fish, of the flour, of the rent, of the shoes and of the medicine, all depends on political decisions. The political illiterate is so stupid that he is proud and swells his chest saying that he hates politics. The imbecile doesn't know that, from his political ignorance is born the prostitute, the abandoned child, and the worst thieves of all, the bad politician, corrupted and flunky of the national and multinational companies.

–Bertolt Brecht

Contents

Section III: Science

Section IV: Media and International Affairs

Section V: Society

Section VI: Healthcare and Ethics

Introduction

The Marxist theorist, Rosa Luxemburg had once said that those who do not move, do not notice their chains. Nothing can be closer to the truth, particularly in societies which 'normalize' chains, instead of neutralizing them. It is thus essential to make the correct noises at the correct time and if need be, all the time.

In my opinion, one of the best ways to create noises is through the written word. When all is said and done, words will survive to tell the story of our times. The rough jangle of the chains which Rosa Luxemburg mentioned, can reach the ears of history through words and hence it is essential that we etch our times on paper. In the words of Knut Hamsun, modernist literature should focus on intricacies of the human mind, the writers should describe the whisper of blood and the pleading of the bone marrow. *Announcing the Monster* is one such effort to put on record some aspects of India's social, political and economic history during the times of the 'Modi Raj', a period extending between May 2014 to May 2019. These are the whispers of blood and the pleading of the bone marrow.

Announcing the Monster is a collection of more than sixty essays written on various aspects of the so-called "new India" which we saw emerge after the May 2014 general elections. This new India, is fiercely religious, murderously sensitive to a cow carcass, unknowing of the poor but knowing of the interests of the rich and the powerful. The country threw many horrors, many trepidations and many stories which were interesting and horrible enough to write upon. The period between 2014 and 2019 saw unprecedented changes in our social and political life. A remarkable change in this regard was the gradual erosion of freedom of expression and right to dignity and life, all under the watchful eye of the regime. The so-called lunatic fringe suddenly became important or was probably made important and it held reason and debate of the land by the scruff of their necks. Mob violence and lynching by cow vigilantes became routine. The secular fabric of the nation was torn to tatters and 'otherization' of minorities and Dalits took centrestage. The narrative of hate was legitimized even at the highest offices of the executive.

With important economic decisions like demonetization bringing a pause to economic growth, the politics of identity became even more essential. Political rhetoric was reduced to ugly rubble and in each state election blatant communal agenda was unleashed on the common masses of the country. Flames of polemics of religion and caste were fuelled not doused as it meant a sure means to secure political power. Scientific temper, so laboriously built over the last few decades, was dented by the irresponsible, irrational rant of the political leadership. Vital people-centric issues like health and education were relegated to the backburner. The healthcare system became an innocent bystander in the onslaught on people-centric development. To say that it is only the state which is responsible for the petrification of the healthcare system would be unjustified. Doctors and other healthcare personnel are equally responsible for the chaos. Many of the essays in this book thus deal with the convolutions of healthcare and the ethics which surrounds it.

Amidst all this din, there were some who held on to reason as it was the only ray of hope in a sea of hopelessness. Still others, like Kalburgi, Pansare and Gauri Lankesh had to lay their lives at the doorstep of rationality. Their murderers having the tacit support of the political class of the day. Some others like Sudha Bhardwaj, Varavara Rao and others were incarcerated for being hopeful and not giving way to fear. Still others like Anand Teltumbde and Gautam Navlakha are being intimidated with imminent arrest.

The book has six broad sections that deal with entirely different issues which the country saw emerge in the said period. Each essay was written in the context of current happenings which left us bewildered, sad and most importantly, concerned for the India where we grew up. The first essay, Announcing the Monster, was written a day after the current regime was voted to power. Some of the pieces cannot be technically called essays as they are either too short or are in a poetic form. As they say, conflict of ideas gives rise to creativity. Without creativity change is not possible. The book has two fictitious stories and one review of a Hindi feature film. These are part of a creativity of angst. The story Dogs and Rabbits was written immediately after the controversy involving the students of Jawaharlal Nehru University (Delhi) in February 2016. Lafzon ka Perh (Tree of Words) was written after an income tax raid at a prominent news channel which was perceived as being anti-government. It appeared that there was an attempt to silence dissent by the regime. There are a few pieces which were not written between 2014-19. In fact both these essays (Our Choice: Arundhati Roy or Insulated Nationalism and Kashmir: Let's Blink) were written more than eight years ago but unfortunately fail to lose their relevance even today. For their germaneness, these pieces have been modified and reproduced in the book. The book has three articles which do not have roots in India (Gaza-2014: When Mourning Becomes Reawakening, Paris Attacks: A View from the Other Side of the Fence and Red and Blue: Let's Make America Great Again) but the reason to include them was the same- to highlight the suffering of humans across geographical boundaries, that is to listen to the jangle of their chains. Besides, the perpetrators in two of those pieces, namely the United States and Israel, are unfortunately now made to appear more and more like "natural" allies of India, a fact which was unthinkable a few decades ago.

I must admit that *Announcing the Monster* is an incomplete book. Some might think that it does not attempt to give solutions. It was not meant to. Solutions lie within the debris of the problem. Let us first earnestly demolish the problem to create a debris. As someone has correctly said, when you find no solution to a problem, it is probably not a problem to be solved but rather a truth to be accepted.

April 2019
New Delhi

Shah Alam Khan

SECTION I

Politics And Us

1
Announcing the Monster

My aunt, a superstitious lady, believed in the importance of days. In most religions, Friday is considered to be an auspicious day. In Hindi it is called Shukrawar, derived from the word, Shukra which refers to the planet Venus in astrological terms and is related to Shukracharya, the Guru of Danavas. The importance of Friday in Islam cannot be overemphasized. Who does not know about the Friday namaz? And then we have Good Friday in Christianity. In a nutshell, if you are superstitious, Friday would be a day on which you hardly expect to hear bad news and so was my aunt who was fairly confident on May 16, 2014, a Friday, when the results of the 16th Lok Sabha elections were to be announced. By the end of that day she was heartbroken. Henceforth, she gave up believing in the auspiciousness of days although she still continues to be superstitious in other matters of life.

That Friday of May 16, 2014, was a difficult day to be an Indian.

I consciously avoid saying "Indian Muslim" because the acceptance of authoritarians through a legalized democratic process is not an assault on Muslims alone; there is much more at stake than mere battering of India's largest minority. I will not be wrong if I conclude that what is threatened is far less than what has already been lost in the cloud of dust raised by the jackboots of the approaching zealots. In fact in a democratic "number game", the conceptualization of India and the essence of the Indian Constitution can so easily fall prey to bigots was unthinkable till that morning of May 16th.

The perils of parliamentary democracy could be revealed in such a flagrant, naked way is what surprises all of us.

To presume that all is lost in the din is inanity par excellence. Remember what the greatest philosopher of our times, Jacques Derrida, the master of deconstruction, had once said, "Monsters cannot be announced. One cannot say: 'Here are our monsters', without immediately turning the monsters into pets".

The perception of the new regimen in Delhi should find meaning in what Derrida had said. We need to announce the monster. Discernment lies in thinking ahead of the enemy. Remember more than half of common Indians did not vote for this majoritarian regimen (the Modi government was voted into power by a mere 31 per cent votes). Remember the tectonic plate, which connects India with Indians, has fault lines of caste, region, class and religion, so brittle that momentary glues cannot hold it together without an imminent danger of drifting apart on the slightest provocation.

The need of the hour is to gel. Gel with Indians who think and breathe alike. To fortify institutions of hope. It is not the time to sulk as Muslims but a time to mourn as Indians. There are signs of hope and optimism all around. We just need to clutch these with all the force and will we have.

As for the dreams sold by Modi et al to a billion Indians, I am reminded of what Hannah Arendt had once said:

"The point, as Marx saw it, is that dreams never come true. "

(Earlier partly published at *Countercurrents.org*, May 18, 2014)

2

Lafzon ka Perh (The Tree of Words)

(This is a work of fiction. Any resemblance to recent events or people is intentional, fiction after all is the step daughter of reality)

Azadnagar was a unique place. It had birds which could speak. Yes, speak as we could. The people of Azadnagar loved their birds but no one knew how they could speak.

The secret of the speaking birds of Azadnagar lay right in the middle of the adjacent forest. The dense forest had an old tree, as old as humanity. It was huge; so big that it appeared to even cut off sunlight to a substantial part of the forest on a bright day. The tree was unique, remarkably different from other trees. It did not have fruits or flowers. Words hung from its branches. Words which made sense, words of love, words of hate and words which made no sense at all. Each branch had thousands of words and in spring it even bloomed, aligning the words into stories. It was called the Lafzon ka Perh (Tree of Words).

Every morning, the birds of Azadnagar came to peck on these words and stories. They pecked and pecked till their tiny hearts were full of words. They then flew to the town and narrated beautiful stories, soul stirring poems and ravishing songs to the people of the land. Everybody in Azadnagar loved the speaking birds and they all lived happily.

Then, a new king ascended the Azadnagar throne. No one knew why, but the new king hated words. He particularly abhorred the spoken word. The spoken word is probably the most significant; after all it is the essence of communication.

One day he ordered the caging of all birds of Azadnagar

and this was followed dutifully. With all the birds gone, Azadnagar became quiet. As silent as a grave. The king was happy but he wanted to know the secret of the speaking birds. An old myna, caged without food or water for days, revealed the secret to his ministers. The king immediately ordered that the tree of words be cut down. He was trying to ensure that no bird could speak in future. Such was his hate for words! A team was sent to the forest with hammers, pickaxes, adzes, mattocks and other ugly tools to bring down the lafzon ka perh. The tree was big and strong and it took the king's men three years to bring it down. The day it fell, the king's men celebrated. Azadnagar became free of the spoken word.

Then one day, a tiny swallow came to the palace parapet and spoke. It was followed by more speaking birds—sparrows, bulbuls, pigeons, doves, herons, crows and even the vultures with their ugly bent beaks. All had stories, songs and words of wisdom for the people of Azadnagar. The reappearance of the speaking birds bewildered the king and he dispatched a team to the forest to probe.

To their utter surprise, the king's men discovered that the place where the lafzon ka perh once stood, was strewn with tiny saplings on which words bloomed. They realized, when the tree was brought down, it had spilled its words all around the forest like a sweet scent. Its offspring now covered the whole forest and words were scattered on the forest floor like dry leaves.

The speaking birds of Azadnagar kept the spoken word alive forever. The king and his men knew that it is impossible to bar the spoken word.

The spoken word was the essence of communication!

The lafzon ka perh had become immortal.

(Earlier published at *Countercurrents.org*, on June 7, 2017)

3

Dismantling India

Every single day we are woken up by new news. Whether it is the lynching of minorities and Dalits or the re-structuring of key institutions of India's socialist and democratic commitment (even how so little!). Today came the news of the axing of the National Nutrition Monitoring Bureau (NNMB) of the country. This was the national agency collecting data on the nutrition status among the marginalized population of the country. Being affiliated with the expert committee on Tribal Health in the NNMB, I was witness to the realistic data and equally realistic guidelines, which the NNMB proposed. In fact the best papers in nutritional crisis and management in this country came through the database of the NNMB. For the current government this was no reason to continue with the apex body or may be, this was the reason to dismantle the NNMB? The absolutists never want to see the mirror!

I am reminded of the story of the crazy Serbian zoo tiger that started to chew on its own paws following the carpet bombing by allied forces (as told by Arundhati Roy). It appears that we are getting to the point where the present government is beginning to chew its own paws in the excitement of dismantling the concept of India.

(Earlier partly published at *Countercurrents.org*, on November 1, 2015)

4

Uncanny Likeness?

At the outset please let me clarify that I am an Indian, I love my nation and I stand up straight and attentive every time the national anthem is played. Having said this, I have interest in history and love to read anything and everything that helps me decipher the past because in the words of Churchill, the more backward we look, the more forward we can see!

In recent times, I have developed a keen interest in the history of Nazi Germany. Why? Well, for no particular reason! I hope this will not be a reason to label me seditious? No? Phew...thanks what a relief! Anyway....

So I share a few facts.

Adolf Hitler had worked as a "causal labourer" in Munich in 1913, a fact, which was repeated off, and on, many times during his rule in Germany. A fact, which he believed, helped him in "connecting" to the masses of Germany (uncanny?). Please note that they never had tea vendors in Germany, otherwise.....

Once established, which most historians believed happened by the end of his second year, Hitler's party workers protested against music by Gustav Mahler and Felix Mendelssohn, who were subsequently banned from performing in Germany (and yes, Gustav was from the neighbouring Austria and a Jew).

The Nazi censorship slowly engulfed newspapers and the radio with the newspaper Straight Path and its editor Fritz Gerlich being the first to be banned. Fritz Gerlich had a doctorate and sported a beard (Uncanny?). It is even more uncanny to know that on December 5, 1930, Joseph Goebbels,

Hitler's Propaganda Minister had himself gone and disrupted the screening of the premier of the movie, All Quiet on the Western Front, a movie based on a novel which was very unpopular with the Nazis.

By 1935 Hitler had realized that to fully control the German mind, it was essential to control the universities. In this respect he suppressed universities which had significant communists in academic positions (uncanny?). The academicians and students at the Munich University organized what was called The White Rose, a non-violent, intellectual group of anti-Nazis. One student of this group was twenty-one-year-old Sophie Scholl, who was convicted of sedition and later killed by the Nazis (surely uncanny).

After coming to power in 1933, Hitler used radio to widely broadcast his speeches. What is uncanny is the fact that the Ministry of Propaganda ran his speeches on a weekly basis on radios throughout Germany. I am not sure what these weekly programmes were called but were surely the voice from the Fuehrer's heart!

We are told that Hitler was a vegetarian although the reasons for him turning vegetarian remain obscure. In 1934 the Nazi government issued a decree banning kosher meat in Germany. And even more uncanny is the fact that Hitler stressed cleanliness of the nation as one of the first few drives the Nazi regimen took over after assuming power in 1933. It was aimed at increasing tourism in the Third Reich. He believed that the tourists should praise Nazi Germany for its cleanliness, orderliness and cultural vitality.

And finally how can we talk of Hitler, Nazis and the Third Reich without mentioning mob lynching? Yes, mob lynching, as we know! The Russelsheim massacre involved the lynching of six American airmen by the people of Russelsheim, a town in the Gross-Gerau district of Central Germany. What is worth mentioning is the fact that the people of Russelsheim killed the six airmen with sticks, stones, hammers and shovels (uncanny?); no guns were used!

So even as my indulgence in Nazi history grows, I can only hope that I discover less and less of the uncanny resemblances, of lesser and novel atrocities, of lesser suppression of expression and of course less of fascism!

We surely don't want to tread that path!

> There was once a nanny goat who said,
> In my cradle someone sang to me:
> "A strong man is coming.
> He will set you free!"
> The ox looked at her askance.
> Then turning to the pig
> He said,
> "That will be the butcher."
>
> –Bertolt Brecht

(Earlier published at *Countercurrents.org*, November 7, 2016)

5

Lynchdia: The New India

Pete and Laura, old friends from Derby were visiting. They were here for a month and wanted to go around and discover the land of Buddha.

"We want to go to Agra and see the Taj Mahal", she said with a mouthful of English accent.

"Hmm...Taj Mahal? That's in Uttar Pradesh, nearer to Dadri where Akhlaq was lynched."

"And then we want to go to Jaipur", she announced.

"Well that's near Alwar, where Pehlu was lynched."

"And what about Nalanda?" he asked

"Nalanda University you mean? That's a few hundred kilometres from Sobhapur where Mohammed Naeem was lynched. And yes, he wasn't alone. There were Vikas and Gautam, the Verma brothers who accompanied Naeem that night into eternity."

"We also want to go to East India. To see the tea gardens of Assam. My great grandfather was a manager there." Laura looked excited at the idea.

"Oh, why not? Go to Dimapur. They had lynched Syed Farid Khan there."

"And how about Bombay?" she finally enquired

"Shh... it's not Bombay any more. We call it Mumbai. That's the state where in the village of Kherlanji, Priyanka, Surekha, Sudhir and Roshan were lynched."

So, we are told that India is changing. It certainly is. It has a new tourist map for the likes of Pete and Laura. A map where lines are drawn with sledge hammers and daggers. A topography described with stones and boulders, solid boulders which not only kill but also crush a face beyond recognition. A map with red water bodies and grey skies.

A bloody map of Lynchdia with a bloodless heart and a soulless body.

(Earlier published at *Countercurrents.org*, May 21, 2017)

6

Kashmir: Let's Blink

To the north of the Indian peninsula, uncomfortably locked between Pakistan and China, lies the land mass of Jammu and Kashmir. To some it is home but to most of us who sit a few thousand kilometres away, it is a symbol of India's unity and pride. The shining crown. Unfortunately this symbol of vanity has been the focus of strife in all its sixty-three years of existence with the Indian mainland. It has been inherited through war and blood and continues to be a painful bleeding sore on India's forehead.

The events of the last few months have further added to the tragedy of Kashmir. The spectrum of resistance in Kashmir has seen a new hue. The struggle for azadi (freedom) has new voices and so do the brutalities committed by the Indian state in the name of guarding sovereignty and national interests. The line between sovereignty and subjugation has faded. They want azadi and we want a hold on this strategic geo-political mass. Who is right and who is wrong? Are we really interested in the Kashmiri people or are our interests limited to Kashmir, the valley?

It is regrettable that as nationalist Indians we think of Kashmir only when the valley prods us with violent protests, custodial deaths or brutality of armed forces/the terrorists. Kashmir as an assimilation point in the mainland of India does not exist in our imagination. Whenever we talk of Kashmir it is ceremonial to quote a racist Persian proverb, *"Gher qahet ul rejal uftand ba sey uns kum gheri, Yeke Afghan, doyam Kamboh, soyum badzat Kashmiri"* which simply translated means even if there is scarcity of humanity, do not get closer to three subsets of people, namely Afghans, Kambohs and the rogue Kashmiris. How convenient to disown a whole subset of people which have existed for thousands of years on the very land which we so proudly call our motherland.

The severance of Kashmir's umbilical cord with India is near complete. We don't think of them and we don't figure in their imagination. Do we care if the villagers of rural Kashmir develop a unique psychiatric illness called the midnight knock syndrome (following late night searches by security forces)? Do we bother if psychiatric illnesses are the maximum amongst Kashmiri Pandits settled in Jammu? How many of us even know that one-third of Kashmiris in the age group of 15 to 40 years have some form of substance abuse? How many of us would stand for the cause of a Kashmiri student who has been denied accommodation in Delhi due to his descent? Does it not bother the economists of India if Kashmir is ranked twenty-second amongst the states of the Indian union in terms of per capita income (at Rs. 20,604)? How come Harvard educated ministers do not realize the perils of staggering unemployment rates in the valley? Kashmiris do not exist on the national agenda. How can we expect assimilation of Kashmir when we have opened so many veins which bleed the valley white? To be honest, we stand accused of injecting nihilism in the valley.

I agree that a large part of the problem has its birth in the Pakistan-sponsored separatist movement of the 1980s and 90s. But what we do not realize is the slow transition of this state-sponsored separatist movement into a full-fledged struggle for azadi by the masses of Kashmir. Cognizant ignorance of Kashmiri grievances combined with an incompetent political class has worked as a catalyst in the process of this transition. The use of force, application of draconian laws, fake encounters by security forces and apathy towards the common Kashmiri by the motherland has only given teeth to the call for azadi. India's sovereignty and Kashmir's azadi are at loggerheads in the valley. The human cost of this never ending war is phenomenal. The wailing of Kashmiri mothers, sisters and daughters has a deafening echo in the realms of civil society across the globe. Mainland India stands accused for this extraordinary situation. Every stone-pelting Kashmiri killed by an Indian bullet gives birth to ten more protesters ready to die for the cause of Kashmir. We do not realize that the role of Pakistan and of hate-breeding jihadi terrorist camps from across the border is fast diminishing. Kashmir, the proxy war with Pakistan, is nearly over; we are now fighting our own people—young boys and girls fuelled by failure of faith on part of India. The accusations, humiliation, tortures, rapes and killings have only added to the ever swelling numbers of protestors who come out to face the frustration of the motherland.

The "ostrich syndrome" of burying our heads in the sand, thinking everything is well, is not working in Kashmir. We have tried bullets. We have played the batons. The failure of force is too evident to be ignored. The monster is staring us directly in the eye. It's time we blink. It's time we think. The ignominy of forceful suppression in Kashmir is now beginning to show up. The bloody trail of the past months should be discomforting for a nation which bears foundation of a non-violent freedom struggle.

The call for azadi can be overlooked but can we ignore the smell of human flesh and blood? It is said that peace is not the absence of war but the presence of justice. The Kashmir valley pleads for justice. The serenity of Chasme Shahi, the blue waters of Wular Lake and the dew drops on the pines are not what makes Kashmir an integral part of India. Beating hearts, free minds, aspiring thoughts and a mist of warm breath is what Kashmir is all about.

(Earlier published at *Countercurrents.org*, September 16, 2010)

7

The Jharkhand Government Should Know, Banning a Book Makes It Immortal

In conjunction with the increase in social intimidation and mob violence, which I think have an intentional common end, the Jharkhand government has decided to ban author Hansda Sowvendra Shekhar's book *The Adivasi Will Not Dance*. The book, a collection of ten short stories, has been banned by the government for its 'poor' portrayal of Santhal Adivasi women, particularly in a story November is the Month of Migrations. We are told that protests were carried out by the locals in the town where Shekhar, a Santhal himself, practises medicine, and during these protests copies of his book were burned.

To violently protest the written word is the norm of the uncivilized and banning a book goes one step ahead into the darkness which awaits such a civilization.

Welcome to the new India: democratic yes, but civilized?

Book burning, or tomecide as it is technically called, has a long and chequered history. It is essential that the common Indian of this new India understands this history and the consequences of censorship of books. Right from the burning of books in China's Qin dynasty in 213 BC to the mass burning of Jewish books in Berlin by the Nazis in 1933, book burning has been the most ruthless form of censorship in the civilized world. Books have been burned because they were considered dangerous by tyrants, or even by societies of the times. According to George Bernard Shaw, "Censorship ends in logical completeness when nobody is allowed to read any books except the books that nobody reads."

The reasons behind banning a book can be multiple. Appeasement of an ethnic group (like the banning of Satanic Verses in India) or silencing an anti-state or anti-cult stance (like the banning of Doctor Zhivago in the erstwhile Soviet Union) are the classical motives behind book bans across the globe. To put it a trifle simplistically, books are banned by the state so that the author's narrative does not find ground in the society it caters to, thereby not allowing people to think differently or to even get a feel of an idea which does not conform to their beliefs, faith, attitudes, likings or deep-rooted societal norms. It is thus a means to control people's thoughts, not letting them wander beyond what is considered conventional. In a country like ours riddled with caste, religion, creed, region and tribe, it is beyond imagination what the correct "conventional" can be. But surely leaving it to the state to construct a "conventional norm" is not only provocative but outright dangerous.

On the other hand, it is also important to see where authors like Shekhar draw their stories from. How are Adivasi women characters like 20-year-old Talamai Kisku (who is compelled to have sex with a policeman for Rs. 50 and two cold bread pakoras) born in Shekhar's mind? Every character in a book is a representation of the times, past or present. Fictional characters do not represent people (though banning authorities often make this mistake), instead they represent the times and circumstances in which people live. So to believe that Talamai Kisku is a representation of Santhals in Jharkhand is a mistake, a blunder to say the least. She is a prototype used by Shekhar to depict the miserable and deplorable state of the Santhal Adivasis in that region. The focus therefore must be on their situation, not on them. We may hate the author for narrating the unsaid, but what other means does an author have at his or her disposal? Creativity is never completely realistic and it should never be. It is a combination of facts and fiction.

Shekhar has been charged with depicting Santhal women

in a negative light. On the contrary, reading the story of Talamai Kisku, I did not even for a fraction of a second think that she is represented in a poor light. Her situation is brimming with incalculable poignancy, making you empathize with her and immediately hate not her but the circumstances which brings misery to her being. She is the product of a beautiful creativity which adds life to her character. To believe that the author has shown Santhal women in a poor light is preposterous, to say the least.

Is banning books an effective weapon to silence the likes of Shekhar? Fortunately, it is not. Surprisingly, books (and authors) are the hardest to burn or ban. You may burn a book, but the smoke of words penetrates deep into the consciousness of people. People may be carried away momentarily by random, divisive opinions, as is the case with the populace against Shekhar, but in the end, there is a realization of the truth. Books have an uncanny knack of surviving the brutal force of the state or the tyrants of their time. Like ideas, they keep growing, just like the winter jasmine which flowers in the severest of winters or the desert rose which blooms in the harshest of summers. Banning a book makes it immortal.

The idea of banning a book is also fundamental to the debate on freedom of expression. The concept of freedom of expression should be crystal clear. This freedom remains incomplete without dissent, criticism (of the powerful) and, to an extent, the ability to offend the sensibilities of common people. To say the unthinkable, to see what others overlook and to write what others avoid writing is what constructs this freedom. My friends argue that freedom of expression should have limitations as it can touch a raw nerve, and I completely agree with them. But what right does anyone have to burn books or ban them altogether, even if they go against the sensibilities of others? The answer to a book is a book. The answer to an idea is an idea. To be offended by a book should be a provocation strong enough to write a rebuttal. Civility calls for graciousness not barbarity, and burning books is the barbarity which has been unleashed by some of the most brutal rulers who have walked the face of the earth.

In a free, democratic society, books should be debated, argued and academically discussed, even if they seem to hurt the sensibilities of a group of people. Dialogue is the only means to defeat an idea. Books can be dangerous and they should continue to be dangerous. They carry between their covers ideas which can change this world. We may not agree with that idea, but that does not give us the right to be the thought police. Books which offend the sensibilities of people are best left for the people to reject. Poorly written books never travel long. The involvement of the state in deciding which book is to be read and which not is the worst form of domination, more so when we are living in oppressive times.

According to Salman Rushdie, "A book is a version of the world. If you do not like it, ignore it; or offer your own version in return."

(Earlier published in *The Wire*, August 22, 2017)

8

Sorry Minister Saheb, I Will Continue to Treat Poor Patients from Bihar or Anywhere Else

Dear Mantriji,

I am a doctor, working at AIIMS, New Delhi, for the last 14 years and have been treating all kinds of patients. By all kinds, I literally mean *all* patients, irrespective of region, caste, religion, gender, social status and even nationality. My specialization has meant treating patients from Nepal, Bhutan, Bangladesh, Iran, Dubai, Mongolia, Sri Lanka, Pakistan, Iraq, Nigeria, Afghanistan… the list is endless.

I was so bewildered to read and see your recent comments on patients from Bihar that I thought of writing to you. You were quoted as saying:

"I have asked the director of AIIMs that patients who can be treated in Patna AIIMS should be referred there immediately … There is no need to increase the crowds here… you know how patients flock here…"

There are certain facts that need to be clarified. Since you have taken charge as the Minister of State for Health recently, it is important that someone apprise you of the facts. The following are also important from a legal point of view.

As doctors, we cannot (and should not) refuse treatment to any patient based on their region, caste, creed, religion, gender, social status and nationality. It is not only morally incorrect but actually illegal to do this. So please do not advise doctors from AIIMS, or for that matter any doctor in the country serving under your government, to withdraw treatment to a section of patients. The doctors are morally and legally correct in ignoring your 'advice'.

AIIMS is the apex referral institute that was formed as part of a visionary thought process by the then policymakers of the country. Being a tertiary institute, it is reasonable if patients from distant states flock to the institute. I agree that at times, there is a loss of gate-keeping in referral practices but then that is not a fault of the patient and they should not be punished for this. Let me tell you that coming to the AIIMS out patient department on a working day, getting yourself registered by standing in long queues and then waiting to be seen by a specialist is no easy task. Your premise that Biharis come to AIIMS for even trivial diseases raises some doubts. I would not waste a day, surrounded by the dying and the diseased, just to be seen for something that could have been treated back home in my hometown. And even if we believe that the diseases for which Biharis come to AIIMS are trivial, the patient's perception is all that matters. It is the patient's right to determine how unwell they feel, unless told otherwise. Perception is a matter of behaviour and I hope that you do not intend to change patient behaviour? If you do, then please don't, sir. It can be counterproductive in more ways than one.

The problem of overcrowding at AIIMS is not a problem caused by Biharis or even by UPites, Rajasthanis or Chhattisgarhis. It is a problem created by the poor infrastructure of healthcare in the country. And who will know this better than you, sir? The serial publications of data on various conditions by your own ministry is a grim reminder of this. The recent data revealed by the Global Burden of Disease Study in *The Lancet* (which is an important medical journal, sir), should be heartbreaking for all nationalist Indians. I am sure you are aware of that. So in a country with poor health infrastructure, and a shortage of doctors, hospitals and other medical modalities, if there are medical setups that are delivering, patients should not be denied entry due to overcrowding. The poor are reasonably intelligent, they flock to places they trust. Please let them continue to do so.

Finally, sir, a 14-year-old patient of mine who has widespread bone cancer and probably will not be alive to see this winter, visited me yesterday. He is from Bihar. Despite such a serious illness, he has not lost his liveliness. Yesterday, in the light of your statement, he wanted to know if I will continue to see patients from Bihar. I asked him to come and see me next week. He kissed my hands with his parched, paper thin lips.

Sorry, sir, I couldn't obey your orders. He had immense hope in his eyes.

I hope you will understand my dilemma and excuse me.

(Earlier published in *The Wire*, October 12, 2017)

9

An Unhealthy Statement

Prime Minister Narendra Modi recently opened a Pandora's box by condemning the allopathic doctors of the country during an interaction called *Bharat ki Baat, Sab ke Saath* with the diaspora in London. The PM condemned the Indian doctors on charges of corruption and malpractice. He emphasized the doctor-industry nexus and shared concerns on the fallout of such a relationship.

The Indian Medical Association and other similar outfits have condemned the PM's remarks largely because they were spoken on British soil, a country where nearly 50 per cent of doctors in the National Health System (NHS) happen to be of Indian origin. For me, that is hardly any reason to condemn what Modi said.

Broadly, the PM is not wrong but to believe that his regime (like his political predecessors) has not contributed to this decay of medical ethics in healthcare in the country is absurd. To analyse the debris of the ethical healthcare delivery system, it is essential to see the complete picture.

The decay in the ethics is the result of corporatization of healthcare by an avaricious industry and politicians (remember, many private medical colleges in this country are owned by politicians or their kin). The overall health market in India was estimated to be $100 billion in 2015 and is expected to grow to $280 billion by 2020, at an annual growth rate of nearly 30 per cent. The disturbing aspect of this statistic is the fact that most of this growth is happening in the private healthcare sector. In fact, there has been substantial cost-cutting in public healthcare.

It was the current government which in its first budget in 2014 cut health expenditure by around 20 per cent. In fact, under the present government, we became one of the nations which were spending the least on its health as a percentage of its GDP—less than even Ethiopia and Bhutan. A report in *The Lancet* in 2016 mentioned that 80 per cent of India's healthcare is now delivered by the private practitioners, the very doctors whom the PM now condemns as corrupt. The destruction of public healthcare in the country has resulted in this extremely lopsided situation and hence the increasing likelihood of the malpractices about which the PM spoke in London. This government, like others, has contributed to this situation.

The Prime Minister also mentioned the capping of implant prices under his regime. This is a welcome step but we were told that capping of total knee implants would be followed by capping of prices of the total hip implants, ocular lenses, and many other such items. Nothing has happened in the last eight months in this regard. I hope the government will show haste in capping prices of other implants as well.

To blame the doctors is easy. There is no doubt that significant numbers of doctors are involved in unethical practices. It is also true that doctors and pharmaceutical companies form an unholy alliance. But to paint the entire profession with the same brush is a matter of serious concern, especially when it comes from the highest quarters.

We live in extremely dangerous times where violence against doctors is on the rise. Such imprudent statements coming from the top embolden those who resort to violence. The politically powerful should realize that the only effective way to reduce corruption in healthcare is to strengthen the public healthcare delivery system. Corruption is not the handiwork of individuals alone, it is also systemic. Repair the system and the corrupt will melt away like snow under the sun.

(Earlier published in *The Indian Express*, May 3, 2018)

10

The Chowkidars I Know

(Names of people and organizations in this piece have been changed; their situations however remain the same)

Ajay, works as a security guard with the Total Security agency (or an agency with a name which was nearly as absolute). He belongs to Bhagalpur. He and his family live in a slum near Seelampur in Delhi. He earns Rs. 8,000 and has three children and a wife to feed. Two children go to a government school. He brought his youngest daughter with an infection of the bone of the leg. The impoverishment brought by the girl's infection has made him borrow money from a moneylender at an interest of around 18 per cent. The girl was as thin as a stick. Besides infection, her main problem was acute malnutrition. After a couple of visits he defaulted on her outpatient appointment. On contacting him, we were told that since the loan was taxing and the girl's recovery was very slow, the family has been shifted back to Bhagalpur. The other two children were also taken out of school. Now Ajay works to repay his loan. And yes, he still works as a security guard, as the chowkidar.

Pratap Manjhi comes from Jharkhand. He owned a small piece of land there and managed to meet ends till his 13-year-old was diagnosed with bone cancer which brought him to Delhi. Initially they lived in a rented room in Yusuf Sarai near AIIMS, but three months down the line their money depleted and the father-son duo shifted to live on the footpath in front of the main gate of AIIMS. They thus became 'cancer refugees' in their own country. With treatment prolonging, Pratap took a job as a security guard at the Ace Security Agency. They promised him only night shifts but in return he signed on a pay agreement of Rs. 15,000 even though he was only given Rs. 7,000. He now works through the night as a chowkidar and in the day looks after his dying son.

At the age of 16, Rekha was married to a 40-year-old drunkard. The man thrashed her black and blue but she persisted with him as she was only 7th grade pass and had no means to look after her 6-month-old daughter. One day he battered her so severely that her two fingers broke. She decided to leave him and move to Delhi from her village in western Uttar Pradesh. She came to Delhi with her one-year-old daughter and took up a job as a security guard in a NOIDA-based Security Agency. The agency posted her at the gates of a posh residential colony. Being a woman, the residents of the colony trust her more than they trust her male colleagues and she thus runs errands for them at a nominal price. She works through the day as a chowkidar and in the evening as a maid for a few households. The only regret she has is that she now has less time to spend with her daughter who seems to be growing up quickly.

"But then that is the fate of a chowkidar, isn't it?" she says.

Ram Singh from Rajasthan brought his 7-year-old son with a fungating tumour of the thigh bone. The tumour was so big that chances of limb salvage were minuscule. Ram Singh worked as a security guard with the On Time Security Agency somewhere in Ghaziabad. He was insistent that the child's limb be saved and that he was against getting it amputated. He took away his son when I tried to persuade him that amputation was the only chance to save the child's life. On subsequent visits, I realized that he would default and not bring his son ever to AIIMS. I asked him patiently why he did not want an amputation. He hesitated for a few seconds and said, "Doctor saheb if he has an amputation, he won't be able to even become a chowkidar like me."

Sultan from Uttarakhand was 22 years old when he had

joined the Fearless Security Agency in Delhi. Five years after working as a chowkidar, he was sure the company was planning to throw him out soon. His fair skin, deep brown eyes and a Muslim name had made him a suspect. Lately the company had received many phone calls asking for replacing the 'Kashmiri looking Muslim man' from wherever they were posting him—construction sites, residential colonies and even corporate offices. His presence was causing anxiety to many. I too was not sure if he was a Muslim.

When enquired if he was a Muslim, he smiled and replied, "Saheb chowkidar ka koi mazhab kahan hota hai?" (Sir does a chowkidar have a religion?).

(Earlier published at *Newslaundary*, March 22, 2019)

SECTION II

COMMUNALISM

11

Me, the Antinational?

Farooque was a Kashmiri. He hated India. His cousin was killed by security forces while at a demonstration in Srinagar. This was 1990. We were classmates; I always took him head on for his anti-India rhetoric. Those were the times when no one minded his orotundity and our arguments, and life went on. Then came March 1992 and the cricket world cup. The determined Imran Khan and Pakistan came from behind and won the cup. I bunked college the day Pakistan won because I did not have the courage to face Farooque, who was of course ecstatic beyond words and wanted to rub salt in my wounds. I was madly in love with cricket and equally devoted to the team which had let me down—but I knew defeat was part of the game, as much as of life.

But 1992 also came with hate. The 400-year-old Babri Masjid was pulled down within four hours by kar sevaks. That become a defining moment in India's secular history and Farooque taunted me on being the citizen of a country which could not protect the mosque from a group of rabid communalists. I was hurt but was confident that this was the handiwork of a lunatic fringe which should never find toe space within the pluralistic and secular India I was so proud of. Again, life went on and we graduated from college. India too graduated from an innocent past and the mid-1990s saw the swift embracing of neoliberal policies. People changed and jumped classes overnight. Farooque left the country and we lost contact.

And then 2002 happened. Yes, it happened not as a year but as a moment of perfidy for the thousands of Muslims who lived in different parts of Gujarat, imagining it to be their home. I emailed a Muslim and a Hindu friend from Ahmedabad asking about their well-being. Both were copied on the same mail. The Muslim guy replied in short—"Alive"—while my Hindu friend wrote, "Ashamed to be alive". I was thankful that I had lost touch with Farooque. The brevity of the message from my Hindu friend gave me immense hope. 'They' will never be able to hijack this country, I thought, but a tiny doubt had crept up in me. Like an insect, it sat over my being, fluttering its wings whenever the doubt was reinforced. Then came 2014 and the insect matured into a dark black stag beetle. It grew two tiny biting mandibles when Mohammad Akhlaq was lynched in 2015 and then grew bigger and bigger as it fed itself on the lynching of Junaid Khan, Majloom Ansari, Pehlu Khan and the like.

The Champions Trophy this year saw India defeating Pakistan in its very first match, but we lost the finals to a resurgent Pakistani side. To my horror, I did not feel as bad as I had when we had failed to reach the finals of the 1992 world cup, which was won by Pakistan. I could not explain what deferred me from being sad. Sadness, like happiness, should have a reason and I was scared to face this reason. It was like a disfigured person looking at his/her face in the mirror for the very first time. Was I turning into an anti-national, like Farooque? Why would I not mind India losing to its arch rival? I assumed that the stag beetle within me was preying on my nationalism.

And that evening my phone rang with urgency. It was Farooque—after 25 years he had traced my number through a common friend. We talked for half an hour, discussing our lives and careers.

"Aur miyan, abhi bhi nationalist hee ho? (So, are you still a nationalist?)" he asked me in his usual provocative tone. I was ashamed—not because he had the reason and audacity to pose the question, but because I sidestepped his question and abstracted our conversation into something irrelevant. Irrelevance, the best disguise for survival.

(Earlier published in *The Wire*, December 18, 2017)

12

Where Do We Go From Here?

A Muslim man is bludgeoned to death in his home by a mob for allegedly possessing beef meat. Where do we go from here?

A Dalit student is forced to commit suicide. The lawmakers of the nation question his caste; his intent and wish lost in the din! Where do we go from here?

A student leader is arrested on charges of sedition without a formal enquiry. His speech sounds as patriotic as the war song of a moving army! Where do we go from here?

A murderous mob of lawyers (and a lawmaker) pins down an innocent, à la medieval justice! The rabid lawmaker desires to have been in possession of a gun to express his love for the motherland. Where do we go from here?

A Police Chief sounds so in tune with the party in power. It is spine chilling what this nexus can achieve! Where do we go from here?

A news anchor, the so-called harbinger of facts, thumps his chest so loud that the sound of truth gets drowned in the insanity of his primetime. He stands naked in inciting violence. Where do we go from here?

Not long ago we made a tryst with destiny; today the shards of that broken dream injure the soul of our nation. Where can we flee from our dreams, however broken they may be?

May be tomorrow we learn that the shame of the so-called anti-nationalist rant made one of the 'anti-national' commit suicide within the iron confines of Tihar jail. Would we then ask, where we go from there? May be not. We would have arrived, exactly where we are meant to be—in a dark hollow abyss of obscurantism and fascism.

(Earlier published at *Countercurrents.org*, February 18, 2016)

13
Fearing the Dead

Necrophobia is a dreaded psychiatric disorder where the patient has a fear of the dead. Like a number of other psychiatric diseases, the condition has minimal hope of a complete cure and we are told that most patients live with the disease. Fortunately, the condition is rare and by all assumptions there would be a few hundred thousand patients across the globe. But can we imagine what happens when a country suffers from necrophobia? Yes, a country! And that too one of the most populous countries on the planet?

Welcome to the Democratic Republic of India.

When on July 30, 2015, Yakub Memon, the culprit of the 1993 Bombay blasts was hanged, we were told by chest thumping anchors and balking government representatives that a closure for the victims of the blast has been achieved.

'Closure' as accomplishment and surety.

The highest court of the land handed this 'closure' to the kin of the blast victims after thorough deliberations and evidence, which I am sure, must have weighed heavily, beyond the 'collective consciousness' of the nation. The pre-dawn verdict was compared by some to the rays of the morning sun thrust into darkness, to usher a new era. A new era, which could have only begun with the extinction of a life.

Accepting that Yakub Memon was guilty. Accepting that it was 'correct' to give him the capital punishment. And accepting that he should have been hanged to death on the specified day and time (as he was), there is something, which still needs pointing out. The Mumbai Police issued a warning to those planning to attend Memon's prospective funeral. The legal warning read that nobody will photograph/videograph Yakub Memon's corpse during transportation. This step had been taken by the police to ensure tranquillity and harmony in the city. A measure, we were told, taken to prevent visuals being used later by anti-national elements to provoke people and youngsters.

Yakub Memon was luckier than his predecessor at the gallows, Afzal Guru, whose body was never handed over to his family. After being hanged to satisfy the collective consciousness of the nation, Guru was buried within the premises of the Tihar jail itself. The fact that the government fears the dead amazes me. Every now and then the jingoist machinery reminds us of what a willing state can achieve. From waging wars to sending rockets to Mars, governments in power have repeatedly shown their might.

How can such mightier than the mighty state be afraid of the dead?

It is baffling that a corpse as lean as that of Afzal Guru and as feeble and old as of Yakub Memon could actually push a government into prohibitory and preventive mode. This necrophobia of the Indian state, which boasts of one of the largest armed forces on the planet, is shameful to say the least. On a closer scrutiny, the present sarkar and its agenda of "hope" appears to flow through the corporate barrel. Be it the land bill, the new drug policy, or the venomous comments of its own members, the government in power appears to have yet another psychiatric disorder. It suffers from cherophobia, the fear of happiness (of its own people).

(Earlier published at *Countercurrents.org*, August 13, 2015)

14

The Colour of Human Flesh

Flowers, clouds, butterflies and rainbows rule our imagination largely because of their colours. Colours make our lives, red is celebration and black, mourning. The abstract of black and white, yellow and green or red and blue is poetry of life. Colours define our identities too. Saffron is Hindu and green, Muslim.

But how many of you know the colour of human flesh? It is lilac coloured. Believe me it is and I know because I am a surgeon and I see raw human flesh every day. So you think it is useless to know the colour of human flesh? No, not in today's India. Knowing the colour of human flesh can be useful in differentiating it from beef meat, the red loaf with yellow streaks of fat. But where is the connect between human flesh and beef meat? Well, even I thought so, where is the connect?

Dadri's Mohammed Akhlaq Ahmad Saifi defined the connect!

But yes, the human flesh is lilac coloured! Trust me!!

(Earlier published at the *Countercurrents.org*, October 3, 2015)

15

Manto is Not Only Worth Watching, It is Memorable Cinema

The cosy and comfortable chairs were a delightful respite from the humid heat outside. Radha sat next to me in that dark hall as Saadat Hasan Manto emphatically reverberated, "My stories are a mirror for the society to see." And next to Radha sat Saugandhi, the prostitute (from *Scorned*) who loved her job. The Pathan saheb who looted the red thermos sat in the front row; Mozel, the Jewish girl who rented a flat in the Advani Chambers was sitting next to him and so was Ishar Singh, who sat clutching his neck exactly where a neat line of blood had clotted. A peeved Khaled *miyan* sat restlessly in Mumtaz's lap. There was Babu Gopinath and yes Sirajuddin too (of course minus his Sakina). The post office clerk and the short story writer Joginder Singh sat in a lonely corner with his wife Amrit Kaur; Toba Tek Singh refused to sit and stood in front of others. And there were many more who had sprung out of Manto's pages of ravishing creativity of angst. They all sat with me as I watched *Manto* in a posh Delhi multiplex.

What do you expect when you go to watch a movie based on the life of your favourite author? A delightful story with intricate details of his life? Or perhaps the revelation of secrets of his life we never knew—that clandestine affair, that one fetish, that missed opportunity. Fortunately, this is what *Manto* is not at all about. Director Nandita Das has neither spilt any beans, nor are there any moments of truth which we did not know about this great writer, but yet Manto is as beautiful and as poignant as a sunset. There are no conformities to the essentialities which are required in film-making and the narrative has been kept simple yet powerful. Das has bracketed the story of the great writer within two of his stories, one each at the beginning and the end. The absolutely beguiling acting by Nawazuddin Siddiqui makes it not only a movie worth watching but also one worth remembering, like the scented memory of your first love.

Watching *Manto* was like sitting under the dark sky of a moonless night where every whisper becomes precious. It was as if each story of the great master of realism tumbled out of the cupboard of history, allowing the viewers to pick it up, hold it in their hands and pass it on to the next generation to store in their hearts with care—because when all is said and done and when we have all perished, only stories will remain. How apt when in one shot Manto says, "*Aakhir mein sirf afsane hee reh jayenge* (In the end only stories shall remain)."

The timing of *Manto* could not have been better. We are living in interesting times (I consciously refrain from using the word "dangerous" instead of "interesting"). In these interesting times of collective amnesia, it is important that we are shaken up now and then. We need to be jolted to breathe, else the festering wounds over our bodies will rot further. The prejudices of our past have started to rule our present with a deadly assault on our liberal thoughts, and who better could Das have selected to make a movie on but the man who is not only a master of realism but also a gifted rebel, the antithesis of the very society he lived in.

I doubt whether Manto can be conveniently called a liberal—he was much more than that. Calling him 'liberal' would be insulting his legacy. He was like his stories—truthful, simple and brutal. Strangely enough, he wasn't a Sartre, neither a Marx and nor a Spencer. It is equally cruel to compare him with other greats of short story writing like Nikolai Gogol. He was just Manto. His oblique descriptions of sexuality, his love for the wretched of the land, his derision of collective morality, and his savage narration of post-Partition violence with no holds barred is what was unacceptable to the people of his time, including the so-called progressive writers, as the movie depicts at multiple points. Of particular note in this respect are the court scenes where the author defends himself against the charges of obscenity for his story *Thanda Gosht* (*Cold Meat*).

In fact, there are points in the movie when you, the Manto admirer, hallucinate that Nawazuddin Siddiqui is Manto. A feeling when you transcend with Das's story and direction into a time zone which surely does not belong to this era. To enter into the mind of the great writer and to make the audience travel with you through the alleys of his thoughts is something which is commendable, and which Das and Nawazuddin have done with the patience of a skilled craftsman.

They have explored the reality of fiction like few others have. Fiction is made from the clay of reality and reality is made of layers of truth and untruth. Good writers pick both truth and untruth to weave a story, but great writers like Saadat Hasan Manto pick the threads of truth from reality and weave stories and this quality of the great man has been sacredly preserved and beautifully painted in Manto. No wonder the wordsmith feels offended by the testimony of Faiz Ahmed Faiz refusing to accept *Thanda Ghost* as a worthy piece of literature during his trial.

Credit also goes to the other members of the team who made this movie possible, in particular, Rasika Dugal, who charms in her role as Safia, the caring and at times cavil wife of Manto. Her frames with Siddiqui were a treat to watch. The brisk character of the great Ismat Chugtai and her relationship with Manto was something which stood out as a happy celebration of two of the subcontinent's greatest writers. Her addressing him as 'Manto, my friend and my enemy' in a letter, was a moment of literary history for me.

A good movie is one which can present its characters in a polychrome, with each shade revealing every aspect of the imagined. In the case of Saadat Hasan Manto, it was essential to maintain this sensitivity of shades. Das's ability to narrate the sensitivity of Manto, the human being, separately from Manto, the writer, is something which is worth a mention. Him narrating a story to his younger daughter and his arrogance at the office of a magazine are the two poles which Das has wonderfully justified. In fact, the movie reconciles both aspects of Manto, something akin to the Fritz Perls' concept of *'gestalt'*—when an individual has the ability to acquire meaningful perceptions in an otherwise chaotic world. It seems that Das and her team had that ability even when they were surrounded by the chaos of Manto's disruptive stories.

We are fortunate to have filmmakers like Das and actors like Siddiqui, not because they can write good stories or act well but because they can make movies which leave us provoked and hence vulnerable. Proponents of existentialism say that there are constructive means against fear, but no such means exist against angst. *Manto,* in my opinion, is a means against angst. Let's put our hands together to compliment the team of *Manto* and to compliment the king of words Saadat Hasan Manto himself. It took 63 years for someone to consider Manto as a subject worth making a movie on; we never know if there is a chance in future for another movie on Manto in this subcontinent because as Jean-Paul Sartre has once said, we are the future to ourselves. And we, unfortunately, know what future we are becoming.

(Earlier published in *The Wire*, September 24, 2018)

16

An Open Letter to Nobel Laureate Kailash Satyarthi

Dear Kailash Satyarthiji,

I write this letter to you with a heavy soul. 'Heavy', not as in sad, but because I feel burdened by the baggage of your recent visit to the Rashtriya Swayamsevak Sangh (RSS) headquarters for the Vijayadashami function. You are the recipient of the Nobel Peace Prize and therefore, the peace loving citizens of this globe unconsciously feel to have a right on your actions. My writing this letter to you is the use of that collective right on the so-called gospels of peace.

Your attendance of the RSS event has belittled the peace prize which was bestowed on you. Imagine Malala Yousafzai, your Nobel co-recipient, going to a function of say Jamat-e-Islami of Pakistan? What havoc would that create? What face would she have if she did that? I may mention that I purposefully avoid sending her to an imaginary Talibani function in Pakistan because the comparison between the RSS and Taliban would not be correct even though the actions purported by the two organizations were for a similar end point: one, a Hindu Rashtra and the other, an Islamic Caliphate.

Since we live in times of collective amnesia, it may be worth remembering that the very organization you decorated was banned thrice by the Government of India. The very first memorandum which banned the organization four days after Mahatma Gandhi was murdered had some remarks which should worry us all who love peace and peaceful means of struggle. The order said, "to root out the forces of hate and violence that are at work in our country and imperil the freedom of the nation...the Government of India have decided to declare unlawful the Rashtriya Swayamsevak Sangh in several parts of the country, individual members of the Rashtriya Swayamsevak Sangh have indulged in acts of violence involving arson, robbery, dacoity, and murder and have collected illicit arms and ammunitions. They have been found circulating leaflets exhorting people to resort to terrorist methods, to collect fire arms....the cult of violence sponsored and inspired by the activities of the Sangh has claimed many victims (sic)".

I suppose an order banning the Taliban in your co-recipient's country Pakistan would not sound much different than this Satyarthi? Don't you think so?

I also know your commitment to the Gandhian philosophy of non-violence. You have always come out as a Gandhian to the world, although knowingly or unknowingly, you have avoided speaking against state-sponsored violence. I don't remember you condemning the brutalities unleashed by the state against the children of Kashmir (most blinded by the notorious pellet guns happen to be teenagers) or even against the killing of tribals in the state of Chhattisgarh by labelling them Naxals. I hope you understand that for every tribal killed, a child is orphaned?

It is a matter of concern that at the very function which you bejewelled, RSS chief Mohan Bhagwat issued a call against the so called 'urban Naxals'. This is a problematic term in itself which unfortunately is used in the present day to delineate those who seek to speak for freedom of expression, liberal values and ideas of a free and inclusive society. I would definitely like to hear your opinion on this jargon of hate and more so when the Mahatma had himself said, a man is the product of his thoughts; what he thinks he becomes. Please let us know what you think of Bhagwat, more so in view of the regular rhetoric of the kind he said at the function. Isn't he the product of his thoughts?

Also, who does not know that the organization you chose

to go to as an honoured guest is involved in the assassination of Gandhi? I understand that in the last couple of years, there are desperate attempts by the RSS and its Sangh *parivar* to legitimize Gandhi's killer, Nathuram Godse. But fortunately, history has a knack of catching up with its characters. Unless of course, they are given a kind of credibility which visits by a Nobel Peace Prize winner will definitely (and unfortunately) bring to their fib claims. I hope I don't need to reiterate what the Swedish Nobel Committee, which bestowed you with the Nobel Peace, says about Gandhi. They call him their missing laureate, having failed to give him the Nobel Peace despite six nominations.

You should have been careful of the legacy of the RSS before accepting their invitation.

I understand that it is difficult for you to speak on all the issues I mentioned in this letter because of various reasons and you, being a Nobel recipient, are not entitled to echo sentiments on every issue under the sun. But you giving credibility to a function of the RSS is a serious breach of trust in peace. Peace and its gospels should be careful in choosing their friends, sir.

We are living in interesting times where the definitions of inclusiveness, justice, equality and peace are being rearranged to the convenience of those in power. Let's not partner those who are on the other side of the fence. Those in power are not more important than the peace which you have been given the responsibility to represent. To share the legacy of peace, I am sure you could have found better and more worthy haulers than the very killers of the epitome of non-violence. In the words of Dominique Pire, a peace laureate like you, to act without knowledge is folly, to know without acting is cowardice.

Yours truly,

(Earlier published in *The Wire*, October 20, 2018)

17

Why I Won't Do Yoga This Sunday!

Ever since the PM Narendra Modi has called for active participation of citizens of the country at the International Yoga Day, I have been reading the comments of various Muslim scholars and organizations on Yoga with interest. I see that the debate is hovering more on whether doing Surya Namaskar is anti-Islamic or whether Yoga per se is a very "Hindu" ritual, so on and so forth. Unfortunately we have missed the woods for the tree. The very basis of the debate on Yoga is lost in the din of religiosity, and this is a sort of victory for the right wing forces which rule the nation through (proxy of) a democratically elected government.

It is not only unfortunate but dangerous that we lose focus on such agendas ushered on us by this government. This is not a matter of whether doing Yoga is an Islamic or Hindu tradition. It is also not about Surya Namaskar (many of us do Yoga with or without the Surya Namaskar). The debate should be on the imposition of Yoga or any other tradition through an orchestrated state machinery. Note that it is the imposition of a cultural act which makes the whole plan nefarious and worth a debate. Having said this, I as a doctor have no doubts on the health benefits of Yoga. I refuse to participate in this blatant cultural revivalism not because Yoga is a Hindu tradition (if we can dare label it Hindu!) but because I cherish the freedom of cultural identity which the constitution of this land has given to me and to millions of other Indians. Not that Yoga curbs or temporarily halts this cultural identity, but revivalism of the sorts which this government is hell bent on unleashing definitely produces fear and apprehension in the minds of common people like me.

The agenda of "one people, one empire, one leader" is what needs to be debated and rejected.

(Earlier partly published at the *Countercurrents.org*, August 21, 2015)

18

Knock, Knock, Who's There? Fascism...

"Who is there?"

"Fascism"

"Fascism who?"

"F-A-S-C-I-S-M......can't you understand!"

"But that was long ago. You are fooling me. Aren't you?"

"No, I am not, although I agree that foolishness is essential for me to survive."

"B-but we are democratic and fascism can't survive in a democracy"

(Loud laughter with intermittent clapping of hands.)

"You are so innocent. I love you."

"No. I still don't believe you. You were buried with the likes of Mussolini. You were long over."

"I was buried but I kept myself alive, like, like ...." (Is at a loss of words)

"Like a hibernating snake maybe, haan?"

"Chalo, call me a snake. But I was never hibernating. I was very much out there in broad daylight. My blood was always kept warm here."

"But I never saw you here?"

"Because you tried to see me with your eyes. It needs a heart and a mind to see me."

"But why in India?"

"Because there are many who love me in India. They love me like they love their money."

"Love you? No chance! We are democratic!"

"Stop this bullshit! Democracy! Democracy! Democracy! Give me a fag if you have one."

"I don't smoke"

"Are you sure you don't?"

"Of course, I don't. Shut up." (A bit sternly)

"I thought everybody smokes in a democracy."

"What?"

"Yes, you democracywallas are high on dope." (Laughter)

"No. We are not! We care for our democracy."

(Another loud careless chuckle)

"Care? Maybe you are right. Your democracy is so fragile that it needs caring for!"

"No, it's not fragile, it's precious. We struggled to win it." (Frustration in voice)

"Oh achha! And then you struggled to waste it, haan?"

"We nurtured it"

"Ha! Ha! Ha! Nurtured it with the blood of untouchables and the poor? Or may be with jackboots and batons? Right?"

"You are so obnoxious!"

"Don't call me obnoxious. I am a part of you and your democracy. I am you."

"But none of my part is so abhorrent. I am me because of the free ethos of democracy."

"But I lived in harmony for 70 years with your goddamn democracy. I was part of it."

"You can never be a part of my democracy. You are ugly."

(More laughter with the smell of cigarette smoke)

"If I am ugly, who cares? They have dressed me up so well. I look like a beautiful wish. I look so much like your goddess of democracy now."

"No, you don't! You are as ugly as sin. I hate you!"

"You hate me? Are you sure?"

"As sure as I am of sunrise at dawn."

"But you never tweaked me when I was growing like a poison ivy?"

"The lunatic fringe fed you. Made you strong and robust."

(Loud rasping laughter. Coughs and laughs. Laughs and coughs)

"So now you blame the lunatic fringe? Hmm... and what if they are not the fringe any more? Can you still dare call them lunatic? They are you and you are them now. The fringe has disappeared. Melted like ice under the sun."

A loud silence and then a window suddenly opens. A breeze rushes in and the room becomes foggy. There is utter confusion, an organized din. Sounds of statues falling, hissing of a snake, slogan-shouting. Bodies against bodies. Minds against minds. An unprecedented upheaval.

A frustrated voice shouts above all the ruckus: "No, it's not fragile, it's precious... it's precious... it's precious... it's precious..."

(Earlier published at *Newslaundary*, May 9, 2018)

19

Babu Bajrangi and the Idea of Justice

In a nation with preponderance for collective amnesia, it is important to re-emphasize names, characters and situations, forgetting whom, can put in peril, the existence of our free thought and the very idea of justice. One such name is Babubhai Patel alias Babu Bajrangi. He is a member of the Gujarat unit of the Bajrang Dal and his notoriety lies in the fact that he confessed on national TV (in a sting operation) to have actively participated in the killing of men, women and children in Naroda Patya, an Ahmedabad neighbourhood which saw the worst rioting in February 2002, leading to the death of 97 people.

I still remember Babu Bajrangi enthusiastically describing on TV, how he slit open a woman and took out the foetus from her belly and impaled it on a trishul. While recounting the act, his index finger of the right hand went down in a clean, swift sweep, giving me some respite that the horrific act might have brought a quick, painless end to the ordeal of the poor woman in question. Bajrangi boasted that he felt like Maharana Pratap after the act.

Babu Bajrangi was found guilty of murder by the courts of the land and was awarded life imprisonment. But that was in 2012, many moons ago. The country changed and we were told that the past sins will be accounted for. A new India was promised and in 2015, with the lynching of Akhlaq we were put on the path which would lead us to the promised land. The collective amnesia turned into amnesia of convenience and the news of further lynching gradually started to drift into the deeper, unread pages of our newspapers, hiding there like a hibernating lizard. In the meantime, between 2014 and 2016, when the new India was being laboriously constructed, Babu Bajrangi was granted temporary bail 14 times on medical grounds. We are told that he has gone nearly blind and deaf.

If this information about his blindness and deafness are true, I wonder that despite the 14 temporary outings, would Bajrangi have seen the construction of this new India or hear the jangle of the trishuls on which he had once impaled innocent foetuses of innocent mothers? I suppose, if the darkness and the silence surrounds him, then it has to be an epitome of darkness which this new India now faces.

On March 7, 2019 Babu Bajrangi was finally given bail by the Supreme Court of the country. The bail was given on medical grounds.

The darkness and the silence won him freedom.

Being an ardent proponent of science, I cannot blame or credit the karma in the sequence of events. A cosy darkness and a warm silence also surrounds a foetus in its mother's womb. I am not sure if foetuses impaled on shining trishuls, suddenly exposed to the cruel daylight and the chilly breeze of February, would be so effective in deciding the karma of their villainous perpetrators. The news of his bail, like the amnesia of convenience, again created no ripples in the otherwise unforgiving media of the day. There were no debates on noisy prime times probably because the nation does not want to know. Interestingly, this new India is selective in knowing what it wants to know.

If the merciless logic of his freedom was any measure of the idea of justice, then would it not be appropriate to say that justice has been aborted, and that too quite barbarically? Probably as barbarically as the foetuses impaled on trishuls by Bajrangi and company? Let us for a moment consider that on mercy grounds the bail is justified. Then what stops the flow of this mercy to other people incarcerated in Indian prisons on health grounds? Remember Prof. Saibaba? Why is his more than ninety per cent disabled, polio-ridden body, not worth a bail? How come he, an erstwhile teacher of Delhi University, be more sinister a person and more dangerous a threat, so as to be denied bail when compared to a murderous thug like Bajrangi? And what about the so-called idea of justice around which we thought that the moral compass of our society aligns?

The idea of justice is based on the perception of fairness. John Rawls, in his seminal work *A Theory of Justice,* has said that all people have equal claims to as much freedom as is consistent with everyone else having the same level of freedom. This is a complex but definitely an important statement to understand both justice and freedom. According to him, freedom and equality can be integrated and thus present justice as fairness. With Babu Bajrangi's bail, I am not sure if justice can be outlined as per Rawls's definition. In this new India, justice and fairness seem to be separated at the seams of their union. These open seams, like open veins, are bleeding the country white. Justice as fairness for few, can not only be troublesome but actually erosive for societal norms. Circumstances of justice once eroded leave a deep scar in the social milieu of societies. Babu Bajrangi's bail may not be important for the prime times of the channels or for the political class of the country, its impact on the concepts of justice and fairness will resonate for a long time to come. The notion of injustice is fatally infectious. I only hope that the new India under construction develops an innate immunity to this infectious disease. Nothing can be worse than an epidemic of injustice.

(Earlier published at *The Wire,* March 16, 2019)

SECTION III

SCIENCE

20

What Kind of a Fool are You?

So in the times of the Mahabharat we had internet (and WiFi), Diana Hayden (who was a college crush) is not an ideal representation of Indian beauty (Aishwarya Rai is, by the virtue of her Aryan skin colour) and Civil, not Mechanical Engineers are a better choice for administrative services because they are after all "civil" services.

Hmm...We all know that the sun rises from the east and we will continue to believe so, at least until this fact is also twisted into something extraordinary! But what we don't know is how the east can also mark the dawn of an 'era of foolishness'. How on earth could the land of the wise Bir Chandra Manikya Bahadur mutate into something so extraordinarily stupid?

I have strongly come to believe that just like the Phoenix, fools, too, can rise from dust, if not from their ashes. And if I can hypothesize (at the risk of being labelled an elitist), fools come packed in many shapes and sizes like candies in a box, each looking the same as the other till they touch the tip of your tongue! So what is important—the colour or the taste? The fool or the amount of foolishness he/she can generate?

This is where the problem of language comes into play. In English, a fool is a fool. Unfortunately, English fails to quantify a fool in words. Imagine this, the English language does not have an equally effective substitute for the Urdu word "*Jahil*"! Weaker substitutes like illiterate, ignorant, stupid, etc. are commonly used but none carries the weight, the gorgeousness and the seriousness of *jahil*! Similarly, in these times of utter but dangerous foolishness, English should somehow qualify and quantify the fools of the world. It will make our task easier, less perilous if not easy! It will help us to decide on a rebuttal because not all fools are worthy of a rebuttal.

Actually, the word fool comes from the Latin word *follis* meaning a windbag or an empty-headed person. Interestingly, the Bible goes beyond the English language and classifies fools into well-distinguished types. The classification fills in the lacuna which the English language appears to have left as an act of sheer benevolence towards the breed.

The Bible defines fools into five types: (1) The simple or the common fool who is no more than a fool. A classic example of this type is the poor Indian voter who nurtures hope and is so easily conned by the political class year after year after year. It is the innocence of this variety which generates pity more than repugnance; an instinct to protect more than condemn such variety (2) The silly fool or the one who gets into trouble by opening his/her mouth. When things go wrong from the words of the silly fool, he/she becomes angry! Need I give an example? Not really! Let's not discuss this variety any further because we live in dangerous times! (3) The sensual fool is the one who rejects authority correcting him/her. The Bible says that a sensual fool is more dangerous than a silly fool because he/she is unreasonable. Hmm, so that explains many of those who appear on TV talk shows (some anchors included!). We actually have a party of sensual fools. (4) The scorning fool is one who has a facial expression of scorn, disdain, contempt towards the authorities of correction. This fool, we are told has rejected truth. I don't know but I have seen him somewhere... somewhere in the Parliament, sitting on a high chair telling members to behave! Or probably I haven't. (5) The steadfast fool is the final variety which according to the Bible is the most dangerous and wicked fool. He/she is closed minded and self-confident. He is his own god. Let's not mention the name which suddenly flashes in your mind. These are dangerous times, remember!

As for my communist friends who recently lost an

important bastion in the East, I am compelled to tell them what the Greek philosopher Epicurus had said thousands of years ago, the misfortune of the wise is better than the prosperity of the fool.

(Earlier published at the *Newslaundary*, May 1, 2018)

21

Redraw the Line

Former Rajasthan High Court Justice Mahesh Chandra Sharma's recent comments on the chastity of the national bird need to be seen in a broader perspective. The onslaught of irrationality continues and we are told by yoga gurus that they can treat anything and everything from a foot corn to cancer. The public shunning of allopathic medicine, promotion of herbal treatments for AIDS and the papers to show the near universal usefulness of cow urine continue unabated.

Regrettably, when all this was unfolding, the scientific community opted for silence, a silence which was more deafening then this din of absurdity. It is this silence which leads to the easy elimination of rationalists like Narendra Dabholkar and Govind Pansare with minimal public outcry. It is important to realize that there is a thin line between logic and irrationality and between faith and science. If we believe (and we have the right to continue to believe), in the existence of Ganesh, we are following a faith. The moment we try and explain him through science, we are not only misusing science but we are also putting a question mark on our faith in him. Faith does not require the reasoning of science and hence we should always keep the two at a safe distance.

The use of science to prove faith is not exclusive to one religion. I find it amusing when my Muslim friends tell me the scientific benefits of fasting. During Ramzan, fasting is done not because it is scientifically proven to be good for the body, but because it is one of the pillars of faith in Islam.

The government should ensure that scientific discourse

is not derailed at the cost of electoral and political gains. An example of this commitment to science is seen in many Western countries which provide abortion laws despite the rigid anti-abortion stance of the Church and its followers.

Promoting science over faith is necessary as the presence of a scientific culture helps in the scrutiny of facts, both ancient and modern. While countries like Japan, South Korea and China have deep roots in tradition and culture, they rank among the highest in studies assessing scientific attitudes and scientific education as they constantly invest in science. Data shows that in 2014, China spent four times more than India on science and technology. It may be worth noting that science provides knowledge but traditions manufacture our response to that knowledge. In the absence of scientific objectivity, societies run the risk of turning into illogical black holes.

It is thus important that no effort or opportunity should be lost by the state to expand the base of science among the people. In India, there are many government organizations which help in the promotion of science. The Council for Scientific and Industrial Research, Indian National Science Academy, Indian Science Congress Association and the Homi Bhabha Centre for Science Education, are just a few of them. The government should make concerted efforts to channel the scientific aptitude of the masses through these organizations. The biggest service which the political leadership of the country can do to science is to refrain from making instinctive statements in matters of science and technology.

To conclude, in a deeply religious country like ours, it would never be easy to inculcate a comprehensive scientific culture, but the least we could do as custodians of rationality is to believe in the sanctity of science, keeping our prejudices of faith at a safe distance. For most among us, faith would be bigger than science but faith masquerading as science is what we should all be wary of.

(Earlier published in *The Indian Express*, June 24, 2017)

22

What the Erosion of Scientific Temper Portends for India

The erosion of scientific temper is the hallmark of a society drifting into obscurantism. Those who babble without evidence against the established principles of scientific theory are the worst enemies of science—not because their words carry the power to damage or dent the principles they question but because they sow the seeds of doubt in minds unaware of science as a way of life.

The recent onslaught on scientific knowledge by the political class of our country is a matter of grave concern. From Prime Minister Narendra Modi glorifying 'plastic surgery' in ancient India to Harsh Vardhan, science and technology minister, claiming Stephen Hawking had recognized the superiority of the Vedas over the famous $E = mc^2$ equation, there has been a blitz of statements on virtually every aspect of scientific research.

The audacity of the carelessness on display in their utterances is phenomenal. It has meandered from implanting the head of Lord Ganesh to the exhalation of oxygen by cows to the chastity of the peacocks. So much so that the political class has even bludgeoned Charles Darwin's theory of evolution without any hesitation.

A refusal to accept scientific norms is not wrong. Being a rational animal, the human is bound to ask questions. But for rationality to prevail, it must also be respected. Every scientific theory undergoes scrutiny and inquiry but not in the language of faith, religion or cultural dogma. Science can only be questioned by evidence that is tangible, reproducible and can itself stand to survive the almost-constant onslaught of new data. It is this immutability that makes faith helpless in arguments against science.

Having said this, it is not unknown in scientific circles to accept or refute an established theory but it is important that all new theories keep themselves open to further scrutiny. This cycle of scrutiny and re-scrutiny in science allows it to grow beyond the demesnes of its understanding, allowing a scientific temper to percolate through the layers of society. The critics of Darwin's theory never questioned his intellectual arguments based on their grandparents not having seen apes transform into humans, as HRD Minister Satyapal Singh recently said. Instead, they based their arguments on the work of other scientists, such as the French naturalist Jean-Baptiste Lamarck.

Unlike faith, which relies on the unseen and the unfelt, science questions not only what it can see but also what it can not.

The current onslaught by the political class against science in our country is dangerous because it is putting faith and religion in direct conflict with science. In a country like India, where a large chunk of the populace is ignorant yet deeply religious, this conflict between opinion and fact can evolve quite dangerously.

The commonest excuse given for propagating falsehood is religious traditions. We are told that we are a nation of traditions, and rightly so. But being traditional is by no means the same as being unscientific. The world's most scientific nations—such as China, Japan and South Korea—are also home to rich traditions. In fact, incongruous traditions can be tweaked by a scientific temper. When science prevails in a society, the social order stands to be strengthened. It is notable that in the West, science has a better chance of prevailing in its conflict against the Church on matters such as anti-abortion laws. Whether such a victory would be possible in India is questionable.

The recent advent of right wing leaders in functional democracies across the globe has seen the political class attack science and scientists with impunity. It is a known fact that science does not go with rightist thought. Science and its spine of evidence both stand erect in the storm of irrational ideas.

Across history, the right wing has always been threatened by science. We all know what Hitler did to science when he was in power. His scientists, including Nobel laureates Philipp Lenard and Johannes Stark, relentlessly attacked Einstein on absurd grounds, using poor evidence to disgrace their stature as persons of reason.

US President Donald Trump's rejection of climate change is another example of the rightists breaking from science for political gain. It appears that hostility towards science is the essential step in establishing an anti-democratic order, where hard evidence gives way to fairytales and mythologies.

To expect that our political class will change for the better is to ask for the moon. The least that politicians can do is refrain from commenting on matters of science. They should leave science for minnows like us. They should remember what the first Prime Minister of the country, Jawaharlal Nehru, said: "It is science alone that can solve the problems of hunger and poverty, of sanitation and illiteracy, of superstition and deadening custom and tradition, of vast resources running to waste, of a rich country inhabited by starving people."

(Earlier published in The Wire, March 19, 2018)

23

Remembering Nehru as a 'Friend of Science'

The last few years have seen a sequential erosion of scientific temper in this country. From the head of the legislature to heads of judiciary, science in India has been whipped naked by theocratic, irrational and narrow-minded rhetoric. The day is ruled by suave and not so suave *babas* and *yog gurus,* who unfortunately guide the scientific temper in the country through their nexus with the politicians in power. This is in striking contrast with the leadership of the first Prime Minister of the country, Jawaharlal Nehru, who was a strong protagonist of scientific temper in Indian society. As believers of science it is thus very important that we remember Nehru's legacy of science and scientific temper on his 54th death anniversary (May 27) because the gradual assault of traditional passé thought on India's scientific environment has caused a major dent on our credibility in the global scientific community. A reminder of Nehru's scientific legacy today is a must, particularly for the upcoming generation of Indians so as to insulate them from the effects of bigotry and jargon of unscientific rhetoric coming from the highest offices of the government.

The cultivation of science and its benefits to humanity were crystal clear to Nehru even before independence. He became the first non-scientist to preside over the Indian Science Congress on December 26, 1937. In his address he said:

It is science alone that can solve the problems of hunger and

> poverty, of insanitation and illiteracy, of superstition and deadening custom and tradition, of vast resources running to waste, of a rich country inhabited by starving people.

This statement is the soul of Nehru's core belief in the ability of science to solve socially relevant issues, like poverty and hunger.

The country which Nehru inherited from his colonizers had a scientific infrastructure which was only meant to fulfil the economic and defence needs of the rulers. There was paucity of an infrastructure meant to harness science to benefit the society at large. His efforts at opening scientific institutes of research and national laboratories of importance were thus an important step towards the country's quest for adopting a scientific attitude. New-born India needed inputs of science not through hollow words, but through concrete efforts directed at building the necessary infrastructure from scratch. Nehru galvanized important scientists of the time and gave them freedom in setting up institutes which subsequently became temples of India's scientific research. Some of the greatest names of the time, including Homi J. Bhabha, Sir C.V. Raman, Satish Dhawan, Nalini Ranjan Sarkar, J.C. Ghosh, Meghnad Saha and S.S. Bhatnagar, were given a free hand in establishing the country's best institutes of scientific learning.

In her interesting book, *Growing the Tree of Science*, Indira Chowdhury mentions that at the stone-laying ceremony of the Tata Institute of Fundamental Research (in 1954), Nehru addressing a gathering of scientists and commoners in Hindi observed:

> Many people may not know, why such an emphasis is being put on science. Why so much money is being spent? Why did I take the trouble to come from Delhi? The big countries have more power while our country has remained poor....If we wish to empower our country, which is now independent, we have to create a strong base—so we can learn the basics... This may not show immediate results but finally result in the uplift of the country.

The speech defines Nehru's total commitment to investment in science even when he realized that we as a poor country had more pressing problems at hand. His visionary outlook could decipher the long-term benefits of such an investment.

Nehru's sincerity to the promotion of science is visible throughout his career as Prime Minister. It is worth mentioning that one of his scientific advisors was the British physicist and Nobel Laureate, Patrick Blackett. Blackett, in an interview in 1967 (after Nehru's death) had praised Nehru's intellectual capacity and scientific temperament in loud words.

It was Nehru again who, in consultation with Bhabha, established the Atomic Energy Commission (AEC) of the country on August 10, 1948 with Bhabha as its head. It may be noted that it was Nehru's statesmanship on display that despite establishing an important agency like the AEC, he could understand the disastrous effects of atomic research. He had said:

> Today there is conflict in the world between two things, the atom bomb and what it represents, and the spirit of humanity. That is the paradox of the atomic energy-sputnik age. The fact that nuclear tests continue even though it is well-recognized that they are very harmful in the present and in the future, because of the fact that all kinds of weapons of mass destruction are being produced and piled up even though it is universally recognized that their use may well exterminate the human race.

Nehru had realized that science without technology was like a body without soul. It was his vision which saw the inception and establishment of some of the most important and socially relevant technology hubs of the country. In March 1952, he inaugurated the fertilizer plant in Sindri and on March 10, 1954, he inaugurated the Hindustan Antibiotics Limited in Pimpri. Five Indian Institutes of Technology (IITs) were established on the recommendation of the Sircar Committee throughout the length and breadth of the country. On the inauguration of the first IIT in Kharagpur, Nehru said:

> Here in the place of that Hijli Detention Camp stands the fine monument of India, representing India's urges, India's future in the making. This picture seems to me symbolical of the changes that are coming to India.

Jawaharlal Nehru's scientific vision can also be seen in his shunning religious and traditional practices. He said that, "science was not merely an individual's search for truth. It was something infinitely more than that if it worked for the community." He went on to explain:

> For a hungry man or hungry woman, truth has little meaning. He wants food. For a hungry man, God has no meaning. And India is starving and to talk of truth and God and many of the finer things is mockery. We have to find food for them, clothing, housing, education and health are absolute necessities that every person should possess. When we have done that we can philosophize and think of God. So, science must think in those terms and work along those lines on the wider scale of coordinated planning.

Unfortunately, Nehru's legacy of science has been under assault in the "New India" of today. The current onslaught, particularly by the political class against science in our country is dangerous because it is putting faith and religion in direct conflict with science. In a country like India, where a large chunk of the populace is deeply religious, this conflict between opinion and fact can evolve quite dangerously. Nehru's hard-earned and precious legacy should not be allowed to be wasted by his political successors. On the 54th death anniversary of the country's best friend of science from among the political class, our venerations to Nehru would be in embracing rationality and science as he wanted us to.

(Earlier published in *The Wire*, June 22, 2018)

SECTION IV

MEDIA AND INTERNATIONAL AFFAIRS

24
The Mob

"Who is that with the dagger?"
"I don't know."
"And who is that with the stick?"
"Sorry, don't know."
"Who is that with the sledgehammer?"
"Don't know."
"And look, who is that with the pen?"
"Oh, he? He's a journalist."

(Earlier published at the *Countercurrents.org*,
November 10, 2018)

25

Peace is the Plot

If you love peace, you need to see the channel Republic.

You can't always wait for peace. At times, you have to earn it. Fish it out of the madness which surrounds you all the time. There can be no two opinions on peace, just like you can't have two suns or two moons. But peace is not about suns and moons. It is not even about the rainbows which accompany the dark clouds.

It's about you and me, it's about us.

It's about those authors who want to fearlessly write the story of the untouchable Velutha. It's about those stone pelters who don't want to be tied on the hot, noisy, bonnets of army jeeps. Peace is also about that soldier who guards manmade borders hoping for a bright future for his daughter who cannot walk. And it's about those half-fed, naked, happy children who live under the mammoth flyover near the airport, which brings travellers home from their dream trips. Peace is about the unknown river which flows underneath the pavement of our city.

Peace is the intangible nothing, undefinable yet attainable like the mountain of light, the Noor which drives man to love.

If you love peace, you need to see the channel Republic.

So, who owns peace? The Republic? No.

You and me. We own it in our thoughts, in our books of Velutha and Ammu. In our imagination of hope. In our individual zests for azadi. We own it in our souls of Noor. We own it because we have earned it through the rivers and rainbows, through the metaphors of innumerable moons and a billion stars. Peace is valuable because we earned it, to own it.

If you love peace, you need to see the channel Republic. Peace is too precious to be left in the hands of the mad.

(Earlier partly published at *Countercurrents.org*, May 31, 2017)

26

Paris Attacks: A View from Across the Fence

Elena Beaulieu (name changed), the twenty-five-year-old student from Paris, was among the 80 people killed at the Bataclan Concert venue. Having been to Paris thrice, I could very well imagine the young girl in her bright pink lipstick, dancing excitedly to the tunes of the Eagles of Death Metal, unwary of the danger that lingered in the Parisian air like a poisonous gas. The mindless violence and murder appears to have a perennial occurrence on the streets of Paris now. Following the attacks on Charlie Hebdo this January, 'Jihadi terror' on the French soil became a reality.

But is it all about jihad? Is it all about radical Islam? Is it all about the 'us' versus 'them', where 'us' represents the triad of freedom, democracy and liberty and 'them', darkness and violence?

It is essential to abhor and condemn violence but it is also essential for the French to introspect. The origins of Friday's attacks do not lie solely in the dusty lanes of Syria or the sleepy hamlets of Iraq. They reside very much in the zones de non-droit (lawless zones) of Paris and the une rues of Strasbourg. These areas with Muslim dominance have been fertile grounds for the cultivation of the jihadi who is willing to blow himself up amidst a group of innocent restaurant goers.

What has the French society done to its migrant population which compelled third and fourth generation children to fall for radical Islam? How does a third generation British Pakistani (Muslim) rises to represent the country's cricket team while a third generation French Algerian happily straps a detonating belt across his waist in the name of jihad? The difference is not in their faiths or the migrant trajectories their forefathers have taken, the difference lies in the glue that integrates them to their respective societies. A paradox of liberal progress, which the French society so sadly represents.

It is strange that in Auberviliers, a northern suburb of Paris, Muslim children take an off from school for the Friday prayers. Strange, because it doesn't happen in any other part of Europe.

It is ironical that Islam is the religion of the ghettos of France. The segregation of Moroccan and Algerian Muslims is brazen in the present-day France with Islamophobia governing every aspect of social consent building. In 2004, the National Consulting Committee on Human Rights of France asked its people how they feel about major religions. Half of the population thought positively about Christianity while a whopping 66 per cent thought negatively of Islam. When asked, "what do you think when you hear the word Islam?" A good 83 per cent responded-"terrorism". A study in 2007 in France concluded that those resumes with a Muslim surname found it extremely difficult to get through the short-listing process for different jobs.

The colonial past of France digs its teeth in its soul. France's imperial conquest seems to have gripped its present too. The heavy immigration of Muslims from Algeria, Morocco, Tunisia and other North African nations is the conclusion of that process. Ghettoization, prejudice and a pan indifference to their problems render them vulnerable to divisive and violent ideologies.

It is thus important to know what radical Islam and the likes of ISIS can do to the peace of the French society but it also equally important to realize what the French society needs to do to prevent this radicalization. As they say, peace is not the absence of war; it is the presence of justice.

(Earlier published at *Countercurrents.org*, November 16, 2015)

27

Red and Blue: Lets Make America Great Again!

Last night I dreamt of Alan Kurdi. Remember him? ...No?

Well, I thought so, or rather I was sure that you would have forgotten. After all it is a human trait to forget tragedies. And what a charming human trait that is; essential to survive the pain-hole that this world is.

It has been more than a year since Alan's lifeless body was washed ashore by the chilly waters of the Mediterranean. Even as we gasped at the appalling photograph of the little angel, it appeared that he was sleeping peacefully, intact in his physical form, as if the otherwise angry waters of the Mediterranean had gently carried the toddler in their arms and left him on the beach for the world to mourn. But that was more than a year ago and a year is a long time. It is a long time when you are waiting for peace; it is an awfully long time when people are dying around you, not by weapons but by lack of hope. The little toddler's clothes were the most striking part of that miserable picture. He wore a red t-shirt and deep blue shorts. Blue and red? Yes, blue and red as in the American flag! Wow! What a colour indeed! Blue and red of the Republican placards boasting of making America great again!

And then as the year, heavy with the poisonous smell of dead bodies went by, it took away the last breath of hope from us. It thrust upon us an orange head monster that plans to feed on the likes of Alan. My heart sinks when I grasp that the year to come will be worse than the one, which slipped past our eyes. The kind-hearted Mediterranean will expunge out more Alan Kurdis from its deep blue heart, Alans with red shirts and blue shorts, red and blue which will make America great again, which will make America strong again, which will make America wealthy again, which will make America safe again and which will make America proud again.

God indeed bless America!

(Earlier published at the *Countercurrents.org*, January 30, 2017)

28

Gaza-2014: When Mourning Becomes Reawakening

Do we know how to mourn the dead? Do we know how to laugh in grief and then suddenly cry with pain that's unbearable? Do we know the feel of the cold nozzle of a Kalashnikov on a sweaty forehead? Have we ever heard the explosion of a phosphorus bomb in the house next-door, neighbours included? How many of us can identify the smell of human flesh-raw, burnt, but still human?

Welcome to Gaza!

The story of Gaza-2014 is the story of four-year-old Mohammed Khalaf al-Nawasra, of the five-year-old Abdallah Abu Ghazi, of the ten-year-old Bassim Salim Kawareh, of the four-year-old Sahir Abou Namous and of other innumerable little angels who were born on a piece of land which they thought was their home. Where else can a five-year-old be most secure than within the four walls of his house? In an era where child rights, child abuse and children's safety take centre stage; we hear that the four-year-old Khalaf was brought to the hospital "in shreds".

Silence is unthinkable!

Gaza of 2014 has given a new meaning to mourning. Last week a Palestinian friend wrote, "For us mourning is a reawakening". It appears that for the people of Gaza, perception of grief is a perception of hope or how else can we explain the sustenance of life amidst so much pain and sorrow? How can we justify the beating of hearts and warmness of breath when there is so much rubble around-rubble which includes, houses, schools, dolls, children, mothers, dreams and hope.

Gaza is synonymous with grief. But isn't grief painful? Grief is fear. Grief is horror. But grief being a "reawakening" is something that is beyond normal human perspicacity. Who cannot understand the anguish of losing a child? How then are the mothers and fathers of Gaza surviving? Grief, as we all perceive, is indulgent and comes in waves. In cycles of depression, anger, depression and more anger. The brave people of Gaza seem to have a new way to celebrate their dead children. Reawakening!

Israel can pound this stretch of 25 miles with more phosphorus bombs. It can further fence up the cage that is Gaza, but the courage of the Palestinian mothers and fathers stands extraordinary. Surely Gaza is the land of the reawakened! Gaza is the land of the valiant! The hellholes of war can have no better extinguishers than those who are enlightened by the blood of their loved ones. The UN declared 2014 as the "Year of UN Solidarity with thc Pcople of Palestine". The solidarity of Palestinians with death and the dead is heartwarming.

(Earlier published at the *Countercurrents.org*, August 2, 2014)

29

Finding Hope for the Rohingya in Unexpected Places

We all know what is happening in Myanmar. Rohingya Muslims are being brutalized, murdered, burnt alive and driven out of their homeland in thousands. A lot has been written and said on the atrocities against these wretched of the earth, but recently I came across a piece that was so good I thought parts of it must be reproduced here. Maybe there is a solution out there—and if not a solution, at least some hope for the Rohingya.

The italicized parts are from the original piece and the 'regular' font, mine.

There was the house which was my world, there was the world of others who were also not free but who were together in prison as a community, and there was the world of the free; each was a different planet pursuing its own separate course in an indifferent universe. Wow, the author has so beautifully narrated the plight of a Rohingya. The other world is so truly different. Imagine the bamboo shanty in the swamps of Rakhine State, the home of the Rohingya child, her world with her rag dolls, before she is thrown out into an indifferent universe.

The Burmese concept of peace can be explained as the happiness arising from the cessation of factors that militate against the harmonious and the wholesome. The word nyein-chan translates literally as the beneficial coolness that comes when a fire is extinguished. Another gorgeous concept, the coolness that follows when a fire is extinguished. Seeing the gruesome pictures of burnt bodies of the Rohingya, I couldn't imagine that a word like nyein-chan would even exist in mranmabhasa.

The word is refreshing indeed, and more so when explained along with the Burmese concept of peace.

Reports of hunger, disease, displacement, joblessness, poverty, injustice, discrimination, prejudice, bigotry; these are our daily fare. Everywhere there are negative forces eating away at the foundations of peace. Here the author brings up the basic canons of this problem: poverty, bigotry and prejudice. How courageous to have said what most of us avoid saying.

War is not the only arena where peace is done to death. Wherever suffering is ignored, there will be the seeds of conflict, for suffering degrades, embitters and enrages. There is such a poignant, ethical reference to the process of conflict in these lines. How insightful to state that peace can be reduced to shards in many ways, most importantly by ignoring the suffering of others. The author is so aware of the consequences of the "ignorance of suffering" (of the Rohingya), it almost makes you feel small for being so fortunate.

I am fortunate to be living in an age when the fate of prisoners of conscience anywhere has become the concern of people everywhere, an age when democracy and human rights are widely, even if not universally, accepted as the birthright of all. Again, an enormous statement vis-à-vis the Rohingya. Yes, democracy and human rights are their birthright, and we should endeavour to bring these to their modest doorsteps.

Without faith in the future, without the conviction that democratic values and fundamental human rights are not only necessary but possible for our society, our movement could not have been sustained throughout the destroying years. Some of our warriors fell at their post, some deserted us, but a dedicated core remained strong and committed. My salutations to these lines. Converting the concept of human rights into a possibility for the marginalized is such a noble thought, and that too when it comes for one of the most ignored people in history. The 'destroying years' continue to annihilate the Rohingya community with such indomitable might that for me, this statement is a statement of hope.

The peace of our world is indivisible. As long as negative forces are getting the better of positive forces anywhere, we are all at risk. It may be questioned whether all negative forces could ever be removed. The simple answer is: "No!" It is in human nature to contain both the positive and the negative. What more is there to say? Peace, like the sky and the moon, is indivisible indeed. There is also a mention of the tug-of-war between negative and positive forces, which is so important to understand the crisis of the Rohingya.

There are refugees in all parts of the world. When I was at the Maela refugee camp in Thailand recently, I met dedicated people who were striving daily to make the lives of the inmates as free from hardship as possible. They spoke of their concern over 'donor fatigue,' which could also translate as 'compassion fatigue.' 'Donor fatigue' expresses itself precisely in the reduction of funding. 'Compassion fatigue' expresses itself less obviously in the reduction of concern. One is the consequence of the other. Can we afford to indulge in compassion fatigue? Is the cost of meeting the needs of refugees greater than the cost that would be consequent on turning an indifferent, if not a blind, eye on their suffering? I appeal to donors the world over to fulfil the needs of these people who are in search, often it must seem to them a vain search, of refuge.

This long statement from the piece is its soul. The concepts of donor fatigue and compassion fatigue are so precise—and then the mention of the 'vain search of the refugee' is so true. And especially true when it comes to the status of the refugees, who no one in the world wants to take in. The world has shown such compassion fatigue towards the Rohingya of Myanmar that any appeal of compassion sounds like the voice of god.

I'm sorry—in all my excitement to quote the piece, I forgot to mention the author and its source.

These excerpts are from Aung San Suu Kyi's Nobel speech, delivered in Oslo on June 16, 2012.

Strange world, isn't it? Very strange indeed.

(Earlier published in *The Wire*, September 11, 2017)

SECTION V
SOCIETY

30

Sorry Bantu: This Happens Only in India

Treating bone cancers for the last fifteen years has made me impervious to death, but there is a small problem with this subset of cancers that can still haunt- it affects young children. Healthy, happy children who were dancing, playing and running till the moment that weird knee or back pain makes their lives turn upside down.

It was a salubrious, pink, February afternoon when Bantu had hopped into my clinic, supported on the frail shoulders of his father. He was twelve years old and had a knee pain, which refused to go despite trying every known painkiller on the shelf. He had Osteosarcoma, the commonest bone cancer known to occur in this age group. He needed chemotherapy followed by surgery followed by another round of chemotherapy provided he survives the first round of toxic chemo and surgical assault. Besides the dangerous cancer, Bantu and the family were affected by one other disease-poverty. The father was a landless farmer from a village near Delhi. Complete treatment meant that there were some chances of the cancer getting cured but a definite possibility of the "other disease" getting escalated to dangerous levels. Anyway, funds were arranged, NGOs were pleaded and Bantu sailed through the first cycles of chemo. His complex surgery required multi-specialty skills and he requested that his leg be saved. I remember Bantu telling me that he was afraid of an amputation, as his friends would taunt him and call him "langdha". The leg was saved and he went for a second round of chemo that unfortunately opened new wounds on the operated leg, a common occurrence in children with poor nutrition. Exhaustive wound care meant a further stay in Delhi and therefore a further intensification of the "other disease" as the father missed on kharif sowing. Convinced, that an amputation would bring an end to the misery unleashed by cancer, he reluctantly allowed us to remove the leg but not before I promised him that the amputated leg would be replaced by a high quality, artificial leg or prosthesis. Another NGO was roped in and measurements taken for a prosthesis. A beaming Bantu told me the other day that he could actually hop on his new leg and his friends from the village could not make out which leg was amputated. He was waiting to start playing cricket and was upset by the fact that he never got to bat. He was always asked to field in the game. His scans showed he was free of cancer.

When last evening his father called me, I thought the boy had started playing cricket and the father was excited to share the news. Instead, I was told that Bantu had died.

He died of dengue!

I was numb for a few seconds. The twelve-year-old had defeated cancer but failed to defeat a disease, which should not have risen to such epidemic proportions in the first place; definitely not in the times of Swach Bharat. Bantu became a statistics in Delhi's dengue epidemic. His breath, his heartbeat and his courage were sacrificed at the altar of a nation that has recently started romanticizing with the idea of cleanliness. A disease, which has direct bearing to unhygienic, unclean surroundings, was to become the undoing of Bantu and those who loved him and that too at a time when we have a government, which talks of Swach Bharat and in the same breath slashes the expenditure on health by a cruel 20 per cent in its first budget. India spends 1.3 per cent of its GDP on health. Compare this to the health expenditures in some of the poorest nations on the planet, Afghanistan (1.7 per cent), Ethiopia (3.1 per cent) and Bhutan (2.7 per cent).

The numbers show the intent of policy makers more than a constant, nagging oratory of hope in a nasal tone. The audacity of policymakers in defending a cut in an already "sick" health budget is atrocious to say the least.

Corpses like those of Bantu are difficult to hide under the rhetoric of hope. India is a complex land where poverty, caste and illiteracy mix in poisonous proportions with disease. The urgency of providing healthcare cannot be overlooked. Clean India lies beyond the realms of rhetoric and chest thumping. Swach Bharat can wait, Bharat can't.

By the way, did I tell you that Bantu was a Dalit? Well, precisely the reason why he was not allowed to handle the cricket bat by the boys in the village.

Sorry Bantu! This happens only in India!

(Earlier published at the *Countercurrents.org*, September 21, 2015)

31

Our Choice: Insulated Nationalism or Arundhati Roy?

Across the length and breadth of human history there are instances when a person can get away with murder but being an anti-national (as defined by popular sentiment) is a crime of the highest order. In Hollywood or in Bollywood, treason is the ultimate epitome of a villainous character. In 2010 Arundhati Roy's essay, *Walking with the Comrades* (on Maoists of Dhantewada) had more or less opened a Pandora's Box. In June 2017, she again became the target of the conventional and the social media for her second novel, Ministry of Utmost Happiness. The novel was considered seditious for its depiction of the Kashmir issue. She has been labelled as a fanatic bohemian. She has been disregarded as an author who describes the problem emotively without offering a solution. In a nutshell she has been criticized, spited and even threatened. Of all the comments on her platter, her being labelled as a rabid, anti-national is the one which makes an interesting read.

George Orwell had once said, "by 'nationalism' I mean the habit of assuming that human beings can be classified like insects and that whole blocks of millions or tens of millions of people can be confidently labelled 'good' or 'bad'". Good or bad? Nationalist or anti-national? The vernacular sounds familiar. As a young boy growing in a Muslim ghetto, I had heard this vocabulary on more than one occasion. Growing up in a middle class, "secular" Muslim Indian household, my sensitivity to nationalism had been nurtured and grown into a robust beast, ready to devour any signs of sedition, treason and subversion. It was very late in life when I realized that nationalism does not necessarily mean accepting all that the state says, commands and orders. Nationalism also means asking the correct questions at the correct time even if this compromises the state's own interests.

We all practise what can safely be labelled as "insulated nationalism". A kind of nationalism which is kept free from external influences and affections. Pure and unadulterated. Insulated nationalism carries the smell of blood. It attracts beasts of all kinds. Human history is full of disastrous effects of insulated, thoughtless nationalism. Nationalism gave birth to Hitler. In the early 1990s, it was nationalism cooked with a pinch of Hindutva which saw the rise of right wing fascist parties in our country. Taliban and their machinery of jihadism is the end product of nationalism mixed with tenets of Islam. Jingoism post 9/11 incited the American people not only to re-elect an incumbent and incompetent George W. Bush but also to support his so-called war against terror. Insulated nationalism is one of the most perfect weapons of mass destruction the human mind has ever discovered. A missile which can be fired without any payload; from any distance. It is an unmanned drone which causes unprecedented destruction in its wake.

The rhetoric of insulated nationalism can be most dangerous when the people fed on it are half literate, half hungry, half clothed and all in all half human. This half human does not realize that even his nationalism is half baked in the fire of vested interests. Day in and day out his mind is controlled by the jingoism which appears on television, radio, newspapers and other sources of state outlet. The ability to ask questions, the power to raise a finger, the insight to evaluate a plot, are all burnt in the fire of this insulated nationalism. The story does not end here. The insulation of nationalism is further fortified by scraps of religion, caste, and region. So, if you are a Muslim you cannot question the violation of human rights in Kashmir. If you are a Dalit you cannot condemn the government's credibility on reservation policies. A Christian cannot raise the issue of the Odisha carnage on an International Human Rights forum. And on similar lines, an Arundhati Roy cannot raise her voice against the misfortune of the Adivasis and the tribals of Dhantewada without being labelled anti-national.

Nationalism is an innate trait which we acquire growing up in a society. The components of nationalism cannot be forced but felt. Nationalism means assimilation and integration of people on a common social stage. What kind of nationalism can we expect from the Dalit survivors of Kherlenji massacre or the lucky ones from the Gujarat and Delhi (1984) pogroms? None. Their perception of nationalism and the concept of nationhood have been blurred (or should we say clarified) by their experiences of the microenvironment they lived in. The insulation from their nationalism has been ripped apart, exposing the rawness to factors around them. In fact it would be outright ridiculous to expect a quantum of nationalist packages coming out from such underprivileged and downtrodden sections of the society which has been denied justice in cold blood. Strangely it would not be surprising if we see the perpetrators of these crimes berate nationalist slogans from the roof tops. Insulated nationalism is surely a strange weapon.

As for the likes of Arundhati Roy, who could be more nationalist than the one who has the ability and courage to raise her voice against injustice, inequality and discrimination of her own people? Who could be more patriotic than the one who fights for the rights of those whom we consider inconvenient road blocks in the agenda of our progress. It is frightening to see the "insect" definition of George Orwell being applied with impunity. Nationalism with insulation is like fire without warmth, like a bird without wings. It is time that we remove the insulation from our nationalism so that our raw nerves could be exposed to what is happening around us and with us. The mist of breath and the warmth of blood spilled next door can only be felt if we have this raw nerve.

(Earlier partly published at *Countercurrents.org*, May 14, 2010)

32

The Quiet Darkness

(One of the most important decisions of the current government was to make the Aadhar card mandatory for those who reaped benefits from different social welfare schemes. Although the Unique Identification Authority of India (UIDAI), which provides and governs the Aadhar number, was established in 2009 under the then UPA led government, its implementation was voraciously followed by the Modi regime. The controversial decision of the government to link the Aadhar number with social welfare schemes was challenged in the Supreme Court of the country, and while a three-judge majority, on the five-judge bench, upheld the constitutionality of Aadhaar, Justice Chandrachud delivered a dissenting opinion. The major argument against making the Aadhar card mandatory by most activists was a worry for breach of privacy of the common citizen as well as the possibility of mass surveillance of the citizens by its own state. Whatever the arguments, making Aadhar mandatory for social welfare schemes like the Public Distribution System (which provides rations at subsidized rates) led to its own dangers. In October 2017, 11-year-old Santoshi Kumari in Jharkhand's Simdega district died of starvation after her family's ration card was allegedly cancelled for not being linked to their Aadhaar number. Before her death, she kept asking for rice (bhaat) from her mother.)

Knock, Knock
"Who's there?"
"Hunger."
"Hunger who?"
"Santoshi hai?"

"You alone?"

"No, Aadhar is with me."

"Aadhar beta you only explain to him. He's after Santoshi."

"Open the door or I'll break it!"

"But Santoshi is not at home. She's gone to school"

There is a burst of laughter, "O ho! Beti parhao, beti bachao, haan?"

"You go away from here. You are mean just like the ration shop owner. Help me Aadhar beta, help me!"

No more knocks. The darkness falls quietly.

And then a feeble voice from inside the shanty, *"bhaat, bhaat, bhaat."*

Silence.

(Earlier published at *Countercurrents.org*, October 18, 2017)

33

A Billion Tutankhamens

It is not about the BJP or the Congress, about Amarinder or Khattar, about wisdom or ignorance. Neither is it about cult or agnosticism. No, it isn't. It just can't be!

For god's sake, it is about us, the 1.30 billion souls and bodies which inhabit this land, and will continue to inhabit it despite the perpetual erosion of the ground underneath our bare feet; a deep sink hole in the making which each one of us has cleverly learnt to negotiate and get to the other side of the dig, till we can, till we are allowed to.

The last few weeks have literally taken us from modern to ancient to modern, and back to the ancient times if I may. It must be something extraordinary to define this nation from here on. A nation, which in the last two weeks, had felt the shudders of 70 innocent deaths, the joy of justice and the hullabaloo of ochlocracy. The enormity of each event left us star-struck (I am not completely sure if they can be called an event, for some it was cessation of life). We were dazed. Like a child watching a shooting star for the first time. We cried and we celebrated, we danced and we lamented, the clandestine schizophrenia struck us like lightning. Each event reminded us of articles of daily use packed in the tomb of the (Egyptian) child Pharaoh, Tutankhamen. The good and the bad stuff, in the same shelf, in a holy concoction for use by the little Pharaoh in his afterlife. We cloned into Tutankhamen. A nation of 1.30 billion Tutankhamens! Each dead but with the joy of afterlife taken care of or at least, promised if not by the state then by a court or even by a brute godman who rapes the hapless of his own tribe.

With each suffering unequally divided and with each betrayal unequally bestowed, we celebrated our 71st Independence Day. Seventy-one years of hope tested by the destiny of 1.30 billion hopeless, some of course more hopeless than the others! The hopeless Tutankhamens of an equally hopeless kingdom, where the children of the poor are asphyxiated blue and the biceps of the strong halt life on the road. A truly glorious seventy-one years of a cycle of anger and frustration followed by depression and more frustration and more anger.

But life goes on. It must go on. In the words of Tabban,

Bahut sakt jaan hai umeed
Yaqeen ho na ho, intezaar rehta hai.

(Earlier published at the *Newslaundary*, August 29, 2017 after the violence unleashed by the supporters of the notorious godman Ram Rahim following his arrest)

34

Rohith Vemula: A Star Is Born

Do not ask me, stars, about the garden of the world;
It is no garden, but a town filled with sighs and screams,
The morning wind arrives there, only to leave again;
The poor bud blooms, but only to wither.

– Allama Iqbal

Rohith Vemula, who was forced to end his life by the casteist and communal forces on the Hyderabad University campus, wanted to be a writer of science. His ideal: Carl Sagan. How ironic that the great Carl Sagan had once said, "The cosmos is also within us. We're made of star stuff; we are a way for the cosmos to know itself". Ironic, because the brave Rohith had talked of stardust in his suicide note. A Dalit in India talking of the stars is a miracle of sorts. The structural violence of the Brahminical society is a sequential crushing of dreams, hopes and stars in the hearts and eyes of the wretched of the land. The conspiracy to eliminate struggle adds to this hideous situation. The poisonous combination of a deeply entrenched caste system and an irresponsible and cruel political power makes struggle whither.

But people may perish and struggles may wither, stars persist. We are told some last a million years. Today, on my evening walk, I could identify a new star in the solitude of the vast blue sky. A star so bright, it made my heart fill with joy! A star so intense, that tonight its energy and zest would lighten up every other star in the sky! A star which taught me and you, that the emptiness of the cosmos is filled by the valour of people like Rohith Vemula.

(Earlier published at *Countercurrents.org*, January 20, 2015)

35

Walking with the Dead

John DeFrain, an American writer and professor of Family Science had once written that the death of a baby is like a stone cast into the stillness of a quiet pool; the concentric ripples of despair sweep out in all directions, affecting many people. Gorakhpur was witness to such ripples recently. As the dust settles on the tragedy, details emerge and one such detail which clearly missed the eye of the national media was the fact that the dead bodies of most of the children were carried back home without any government assistance. Bahadur Nishad carried the body of his four-year-old son Deepak on his motorcycle. The painter tells us that Deepak loved motorbikes.

Ever since Dana Manjhi, the man from Kalahandi district of Odisha, carried the body of his wife on his shoulders from the hospital, there has been a surge of similar incidents reported from across the country. In 2017 alone, more than a dozen such incidents have been reported so far. Besides being visually repugnant, the process also carries a risk of transmission of diseases and physical damage to the body.

In the West, transporting the dead from hospitals follows laid down standard operational protocols (SOPs). An extensive enquiry into the Indian healthcare reveals the complete absence of such protocols. It can be easily seen that illiteracy, poor health administration and social norms are barriers. But this should not deter the government from at least developing and promoting SOPs for those who die within the confines of a government set up. Most importantly, such SOPs should not be confused with the legal protocols for transporting the dead, which do exist in the country and, like many other laws, are devoid of the necessary sense of compassion and care.

It is interesting to note that most people who took this walk of shame were from the most marginalized sections of society, both in terms of economic status and social strata. This should raise a red flag with the state in general and the health authorities in particular. It appears that the lack of hearse protocols hurts the underprivileged sections the most. Poverty, coloured by caste and creed, makes a dangerous concoction in such cases. No wonder many of these cases have been reported from the most backward areas of the country.

Besides the absence of SOPs for the transportation of the dead, there appears to be an acute shortage of hearse vehicles which could be used for the easy transport of dead bodies from hospitals. It is common knowledge that most dead bodies in India are transported using private vehicles like vans and ambulances. We are probably the only nation in the world which transports our dead in ambulances. Ambulances are not meant for the dead, they are for the dying.

On June 12, 2016, this newspaper reported that officials from Chandigarh's three main hospitals, Government Multi Specialty Hospital, Sector 16, Government Medical College and Hospital and PGI, confirmed that none of them has a hearse van which is equipped with a freezer to prevent decomposition. If the situation is so dire in a big (and rich) city like Chandigarh, we can imagine the situation in the rural hinterlands of the country. There is no national data available on the demand and number of hearse vehicles in the country even when schemes like the Member of Parliament Local Area Development Scheme (MPLADS) allow the purchase of hearse vehicles for district hospitals.

Death, unlike life, does not distinguish between the rich and the poor. Another aspect of transportation of dead bodies is the practice of long distance transport which needs the body to be embalmed for the journey. Such transportation is essential in a big country like ours where higher referral medical centres are few and scattered. A case report in the Indian Journal of Clinical Anatomy and Physiology in December 2016 highlighted the fact that there are no provisions which deal with funeral embalming in the many (contemporary) Anatomy Acts enacted in the country. This shows that there is an urgent need to formulate guidelines for transportation of embalmed bodies by air, rail and road.

Thus, the need of a national hearse policy with a minimum corpus for transportation and cremation of dead bodies cannot be overemphasized. Developing protocols for the transportation of dead bodies from government and private hospitals with dignity is the duty of the state.

In The Ministry of Utmost Happiness, Arundhati Roy enquires, where do birds go to die? We really don't know where the birds go to die, but they are surely more civilized than us. They don't display their dead to the public in a way some of our fellow citizens are forced to. Death is the necessity of life, it is high time the government should wake up to the reality of a dignified death to its citizens.

(Earlier published as an OpEd in
The Indian Express, August 31, 2017)

36

Tubeless Tyres and Soulless Bodies

Tubeless tyres are a great discovery; a marvel of sorts. They claim you can run for fifty odd kilometres even after the tyre is punctured. I had other reasons to enjoy the boon of the tubeless tyre. A month back air pressure in one of the tyres of my sedan went low. On my way to work I stopped at the local puncture shop to get it re-inflated. I live in NOIDA, the eastern suburb of Delhi, across the quiet flowing Yamuna. The suburban township is situated in a corner of Delhi and on the map appears to be a small sleeping animal, perpetually hibernating from the noise and lights of the mad city.

The shop owner was a local, a hefty, loud man. His errand boy was ten or may be twelve years old, a couple of years older than my son. The little boy looked sad as he sat on his haunches to re-inflate the front (driver side) tyre of my car. Sitting in the air conditioned sedan, I watched as he slowly adjusted the nozzle of the air pump on to the tyre. The morning sunrays filtered through the leaves of the nearby neem tree to dance on his dirty cheeks as if teasing him. Grease and soot formed a black line around all the nails of his fingers and toes like a wooden frame enveloping a precious painting. The sudden hissing sound of the rushing air had little effect on his dull demeanour. His tiny fingers barely held on to the pump nozzle as the back flowing air created turbulence, making the nozzle move out violently. Once done, he applied a little bubble of saliva and the tyre valve was cleared of any leaks. He raised himself up and came up to my window which I had lowered now. Our eyes met for the first time. There was a sadness in his eyes which was beyond words. He had a round face with deep black eyes. His long eye lashes were curved at perfect angles. His hair had specks of brown, a sign of poor nourishment.

"Ho gaya", (it's done) he said gloomily. His brittle voice revealing the childish tone.

I paid some change and proceeded. In a couple of days I felt that the same tyre had deflated again. I re-visited the same shop, the same time and the same sad figure re-inflated the tyre. My subsequent visits over a week revealed that he was Ashish from Bulandshehar, a neighbouring town. His father, who was a landless labourer had died a year ago and the family children were prematurely put to work for a sustained livelihood. There were two elder sisters and a younger brother besides Ashish. Having struck a rapport with the little boy, I was tempted not to get the suspected puncture of the tyre repaired. The repair would have disturbed my regular routine of meeting Ashish. And the tubeless tyre meant that I could carry on for some more time.

Although I could very well understand his circumstances, the middle class 'baggage' of 'doing good' and standing up for a 'social' cause prompted me one day to question the hefty shop owner.

"Don't you think he is too young to work? Shouldn't he be studying?" I reluctantly framed my question, knowing how rude and uncouth the locals of NOIDA can be.

"Arey saab, bachon ki aatma maar do to een ko burra nahi lagta kaam karna. Ees ki bhee samjho aatma mar chuki hai, ab ees ki training lagbhag poori hai!" (Sir, if we can kill the soul of a child they don't feel bad while working. His soul is in the process of being killed; soon his training will be complete) he answered, and laughted throatily.

I was left speechless as Ashish re-inflated the tyre once again, rose from his haunches and said, "ho gaya" (it's done).

(Earlier published at *Countercurrents.org*. November 19, 2016)

37

Padmawati, the Queen

Padmawati was all dressed up for the occasion, a red sari with an equally red blouse and a small ghunghat that carefully covered the charm of her dark face. A small nose ring which curved and curled into a *nathuri* stuck on to her right nostril. The two artificial garnets of her *nathuri* glittered in the sunlight. Three blackish-grey tattoo dots adorned her well chiselled chin. The three dots configured on the chin like the 'therefore' sign, an expression of conclusion. A conclusion which is mathematically drawn and inferred.

Her big beautiful eyes looked bigger within the boundaries of the jet-black kohl which was applied uncaringly. Her hair was neatly done. The central parting was dead central and it prominently displayed a red line of commitment. She had spring in her strides and a determination in her voice. Her tall frame cast a dark silhouette as she walked against the orange sun of that winter morning. She had an amused look, the one that children have when they see a bewildering trick of a magician. She giggled and talked. Her voice had the innocence of life. She was surrounded by an equally enthusiastic crowd, which was as conclusive as the 'therefore' tattoo on her chin. They were similarly determined and equally mesmerizing. Their clenched fists rose in unison, pumping the air as if to break the sky or may be to snuff off the sun. Her careless charm and the determined will made her the queen that she was/is—Padmawati, the Queen.

This was her conclusion like the therefore sign, mathematical and precise. She walked with the three hundred thousand farmers who thronged the Ram Lila ground in Delhi demanding a waiver of their slayer loans. But no one cared for her parched lips and the malnourished baby who stuck to her bosom sucking the last remnants of liquid hope. No television channel covered her, no newspaper showed her pictures and ironically no Sena demanded justification of her wretched being or the correctness of the sad history she bore on her soul! She was the 'therefore' which we all need to conclude and decide. Since she and the likes exist, 'therefore' we need to stop and ponder—where do we want to take this nation of Padmawatis?

(Earlier published at the *Countercurrents.org*,
November 23, 2017

38

What the Celebration of Asian Games Medalists Tells Us About Indian Society

In the just concluded Asian Games at Jakarta-Palembang, India finished eighth with their best ever medals tally. This should be lauded. What is worrying, however, is the focus on some athletes who come from humble backgrounds and achieved what was considered impossible for their social class, because of the absence of training, equipment and other requirements necessary for achieving excellence in sports.

The internet has been alight with stories of athletes like Swapna Barman, Dharun Ayyasamy, Hima Das, Vismaya Velluva Koroth and Dutee Chand, enumerating the hardships they faced, the poverty they fought and yet pursued their dream of making it big on the international sports scene. These star performers overcoming social stockades is nothing less than a miracle, more so in a country which thrives on inequality and biases of caste and class. We should all put our hands together and give them a standing ovation.

Having said this, appreciation of overcoming social misfortune by some athletes—as is visible in conventional and social media—needs deeper evaluation.

As a member of civil society, this applause for the disadvantaged makes me worried, if not derisive. In his book, *Racism and White Denial in the Age of Obama*, American thinker Tim Wise coined a term, "enlightened exceptionalism". The book, written soon after Obama had just been elected as the first black President of the US, Wise says this 'enlightened exceptionalism' is in itself a kind of racism (Racism 2.0). This type of racism allows for and even celebrates individual persons of colour, but only because those individuals generally are seen as different from a less appealing, or even pathological black or brown rule. He feels that "enlightened exceptionalism manages to accommodate individual people of colour, even as it continues to look down upon the larger mass of black and brown America with suspicion, fear, and contempt, suggests the fluid and shape-shifting nature of racism."

Applying the same logic of enlightened exceptionalism and of shape-shifting racism to the Indian society, we can explain the appreciation of many stereotypes which are thrown upon us year after year. Every year, we are made to feel awed at stories of people from humble and disadvantaged backgrounds making it big on the national or the international scene. Remember the Dalit girl who topped the civil services exams? Or the daughter of that ragpicker who made it to IIM? The young Kashmiri girl who made it big in kickboxing? That blind boy who made it to the medical entrance exams? In the same vein, underprivileged athletes who made the country proud at the Asian Games 2018.

The enlightened 'exceptionalists' of Wise are plenty in India, probably because the fault lines of the Indian society are far larger and deeper than in America. Our social chasms intersect at multiple points and each point needs a new icon from the amongst the poor, minorities, Schedule Tribes, Dalits and women to lessen our guilt of having failed them through the years.

The privileges of caste, capital and religion in India outweigh an individual's efforts and hence, when somebody can overcome these to shine, be it sports, education, profession, or politics, we are quick to applaud. This applause is not for the group to which the person belongs. That group still remains an unworthy entity. It is only for the individual who could fight his/her way up from the depths in which that group survives.

Those appreciating the 'exceptionalists' are indifferent

towards the fate of Dalits, minorities or disabled. So while appreciating the Dalit civil services topper, the privileged do not feel the need to contribute towards providing equal opportunities for Dalits. On the contrary, there is a constant bid to thwart efforts towards inclusiveness (remember that anti-reservation rhetoric we constantly hear?). Similarly, while appreciating the kickboxing champion from Kashmir, houses are denied to Kashmiris in Delhi. The fear and contempt for Kashmiri Muslims thrives unabated. Such is the case with all those bright stars of a dark sky, who are picked up from among the rubble of the wretched and are put in a glass showcase as a measure of civility. There can't be a more hypocritical position than this.

Appreciation of well-performing individuals, which ever strata of society they come from, is not unwarranted. Appreciation of those who have defeated biases of the society is also justified, but it fails us when we look down upon the very group this individual hails from. So should we stop applauding those who have overcome the hardships of their fate and excelled? Not at all. What is required is not picking up individuals as stars from a deprived group. The solution lies in ending the exception.

(Earlier published in *The Wire*, September 5, 2018)

39
Heart of Hunger

I don't know if you came across a piece of news from Kolhapur, Maharashtra, published a few days ago in several national dailies. No wonder you might have missed it, it was (purposely) snug in one tight corner of most papers like a hibernating animal, meant to be left untouched. Well, the news was that a twenty-seven-year-old, hungry man, Sunil Kuchakurni, returned to his neighbourhood drunk and requested food from a neighbour who refused. Next, he went home and asked his mother for food. With no food in the house, the mother-son had a fight and Sunil killed his mother. He then opened her chest and ate her heart with chutney and pepper. Yes, with chutney and pepper.

Nothing more appalling could have been written or read in recent times. Nothing more gruesome could have been undertaken! Absolutely Nothing!

I was stunned for a good few minutes after reading the news and it took me a few days to sleep without thinking of Sunil Kuchakurni, his mother, her heart and his hunger. Which animal (and I use the word animal on purpose), in the whole animal kingdom would eat its mother's heart even in a state of total inebriation and hunger? None. Or at least none to the best of my knowledge. We are told that a species called Tiger Salamander, a north American amphibian, can have a larva which can either evolve into a normal adult variety or develop into a cannibal morph larva which can eat its own species, mothers included. Research shows that this cannibal form develops in response to unknown environmental stimuli. In Sunil Kuchakurni's case, we probably know the stimulus which caused the treacherous mutation.

The horrifying incident raises many questions for the 'civil' society of this country to ponder on. To be 'civil' is to be shaken to the core of your foundations of consciousness by incidents like the one in question. Deciphering the events, it is difficult to ignore any component of the act—the psychosis, alcohol, anger and hunger. Amongst these, it is hunger which stands out like an obnoxious sin (not on his part, but on part of us, the civil society). For me, hunger could be the single most important tool for such heinous mutations. We know people under alcohol or anger commit most odious of crimes but I have never heard anything of this nature. To be hungry is to be vulnerable.

Despite years of rising Sensex and bullish markets, hunger continues to haunt the country like an evil curse. The 2016 Global Hunger Index (GHI) has placed India in the group of 50 countries with an "alarming" Hunger situation. At a GHI of 28.5 we are worse than some of the poorest nations on the planet and rank 97 in this "elite" list of shame which includes a total of 118 countries, a large number of which are known zones of conflict and hence their hunger population can be explained. It is even more painful that all countries of the subcontinent (except Pakistan) rank better than us in the list. A deeper analysis reveals that undoubtedly hunger mainly affects children, but adults too are vulnerable to hunger in high numbers particularly in 'hunger endemic' regions like India where social safety nets are either absent or strikingly dysfunctional. It is important to note that the United Nations declares famine when more than 20 per cent of the population has less than 2100 kilocalories of food per day or/and malnutrition is seen in more than 30 per cent of children and/or there are 2 deaths per 10000 people due to hunger. In India around 30 per cent population has access to less than 2100 kilocalories per day and 44 per cent children under the age of 5 years are underweight thereby qualifying for the criteria for famine. But famines are more political than we think and can only be declared by the government. Thus, the absence of a famine is not its actual absence on the ground but convenient and tacit ignorance of its presence. In the words of doctor-activist, Dr. Binayak Sen, India is in a state of "stable chronic famine" and rightly so. Hunger is known to result in stunting of growth and as per the Global Hunger Report, one in three children in India are stunted due to malnutrition. A total of 38.75 per cent of children under the age of 5 years are stunted due to lack of food in our country.

The problem of hunger is best conquered by a determined political will. Governmental apathy is an addendum to the problem and its subsequent ill effects like stunting of growth. The solution lies in actually increasing the calorie intake of the vulnerable population. The means to do so are many but political willingness is the first step in achieving the target to eliminate hunger. Political will to increase calorie intake takes a beating when the contrary is revealed. The 2015-16 data from the Food Corporation of India revealed that 3000 tons of foodgrains were damaged during storage. To waste food in a country where hunger mutates humans to eat their mothers' hearts is an even bigger sin.

Besides non-availability of adequate food, which is a multifactorial indicator of hunger state, poor accessibility to food also adds to food insecurity in this country. Incidence of poverty directly indicates the extent to which food is accessible and hence with rising levels of poverty, food accessibility is significantly compromised. Poor public distribution system and an absence of social security further complicates the issue in India.

Sunil Kuchakurni may be a symbol of utter disgust and hatred for most of us but his hunger is a message for those who occupy seats of power. A mother's heart is too benevolent, filled with love and compassion for the world. We need to protect their tender hearts. We need to protect the likes of Sunil Kuchakurnis of our country from mutating into the cannibal larvae of Tiger Salamanders. It is high time the government should realize that a hungry population is more dangerous than the most ferocious of hounds.

(Earlier published at *Countercurrents.org*, September 8, 2017)

40

With Love from Gorakhpur

Then they reached, seventy of them,
In shrouds as white as the lilies of the field.
They cried, they wailed, they gasped for air,
Their caring mothers left behind.
A man with a skin made from light,
His gentle look and the magic wand.
He tried his best to make them smile,
His tricks failed, his magic wanting.
It all but failed to make them beam,
The little angels still searched for their mothers.
And then there came a group as white as their shrouds,
A group led by an old man with no teeth.
He had no teeth but his smile was sweet,
As sweet as mother's love.
His naked chest bore three holes, full of light,
White and soft, a light of hope.
And along with him came an old lady,
Her wrinkled skin was clear like truth.
She wore a white sari with a blue border,
And they all called her mother.
The old man with a chest of light jested with the tiny angels,
And the mother put them to sleep, one by one.
She sang a lullaby from the years gone by,
And then seventy of them slept in peace.
Their tiny chest not wanting for air,
Their cold hands not searching for mothers.
In shrouds as white as the lilies of the field.

(Earlier published at *Countercurrents.org*, August 13, 2017 following the death of children in a government hospital in Gorakhpur due to lack of oxygen cylinders)

41

The Dogs and the Rabbits

This story is a work of fiction and any resemblance to a place, person or event is purely coincidental and unintentional. (I dare not!)

Once upon a time, a few hundred thousand years ago, there was a land called, Sochistan (the thinking nation). This was before the ugly cycle of evolution transformed animals into humans. All kinds of animals lived in Sochistan for centuries. The wild boars, the talkative parrots, the ugly blob fishes (who were actually the original inhabitants of Sochistan) and the beautiful deer. They lived with their own dreams, their own ideas and in their own territories. They fought and killed each other but every time they killed, they thought. Thoughts of remorse and compassion brought temporary peace to Sochistan and they continued to live together.

Sochistan had inhabitants, so it was but natural that it had a ruler, the king. The animals elected the king once every five years. It happened that the animals of Sochistan once elected a lame duck to power. She ruled by proxy for some years but soon the animals became wary of her rule and decided to change their rex. The pack of dogs, which lived across the holy river, saw this as their chance to become the rulers. They barked and howled every night and convinced the animals that they were keeping vigil from foreign invaders and evil insiders. The animals were mesmerized by their persuasions and soon the dogs became the rulers. One amongst them was crowned the king. He was big and handsome with a broad chest and a white fur, as pure as the winter snow. He barked with conviction and all the animals had firm faith in him. Soon after he took over, his friends, the hounds, became very assertive. They started troubling the smaller animals. The poor blob fishes, who lived in a dirty pond, were the worst affected. Every morning the hounds would collect at the pond, teasing the blob fishes, pulling them out of water, smacking and slapping them with their sharp paws and even killing them with impunity. None of the animals came to help the blob fishes because they were ugly.

At one end of the jungle lived the rabbits. They were soft-hearted and worked all day, learning and teaching. Animals of Sochistan respected them for their intellect and scholarly abilities. Having done with the blob fishes, the hounds now decided to bother the rabbits. In witness of the monkeys and parrots from treetops overlooking the river, every morning the hounds chased the rabbits. The lucky ones outran their perpetrators while the not-so-lucky were shredded to pieces by the ferocious hounds. Tiny white furs stained red with blood now lay scattered on the riverbank.

Worried and frightened, the rabbits called a meeting. How could they outrun their murderers and save their lives? An old rabbit in the group stood up and spoke. He said, "You will be judged by history not with your ability to outrun the hounds, but by your courage to face and fight them. Sochistan has always given you the freedom to think, don't let them take away this freedom from you. Think and fight. Nothing can defeat a mind which has decided to fight".

Next morning the treetops overlooking the river were buzzing with activity. The monkeys howled and clapped, the parrots chirped with excitement and the sparrows sang happily as they witnessed the unthinkable! The red beerbahutis, the tinniest of all creations of Sochistan, flapped their wings in ecstasy.

On the banks of the holy river, a rabbit was chasing a dog.

(Earlier published at the *Countercurrents.org*, February 25, 2016)

42

The War Has a Name and a Face

The news of an Indian Air Force pilot being captured by Pakistan had been playing on TV channels through the day. Late in the afternoon a video of Wing Commander Abhinandan Varthaman surfaced and went viral on social media. He was dignified and calm in his incarceration, something that stuck to my consciousness. His graceful being kept playing in my mind as I drove back home from work, the setting sun in my eyes. Everything around me looked normal—old people on an evening walk, children playing in neighbourhood parks, discussions in tea stalls, ruminating cows right in the middle of the road. This did not look like a country preparing for war.

Darkness slowly enveloped the city and with it came news anchors—hordes of news anchors. Noisy, loud, uncouth and unreasonable. Most, if not all, wanted a full-fledged war with Pakistan. Whimpers of peace were dismissed as moral cowardice. Most, if not all, wanted an eye for an eye even as their shows had to go into advertisement breaks that ironically had promotions of the Swach Bharat Abhiyan with Gandhiji's spectacles on display. Some even ran live shows from the lawns of India Gate and some from Rajiv Chowk, with hot-headed mobs pushing and shoving for camera space. The angry mobs called for annihilation of Pakistan from the map of the subcontinent, their demand endorsed by army veterans who were present in plenty. There were so many alpha males on TV shows that a river of testosterone could have easily run through the streets of Delhi that evening. War was being sold with ferocious intensity and unfortunately there were many willing buyers. The world's largest democracy was ploughing the fields of war and preparing its citizenry for a spectacle of a lifetime. The much awaited war and annihilation of Pakistan was finally home.

Switching off the noisy anchors, I returned to my thoughts where Abhinandan Varthaman still played hide and seek. His father, mother, wife, child, friends—what were they feeling right now? Can we even come close to his parents' trepidations on the fate of their brave son? Suddenly this war had a name and a face for me. It was Abhinandan Varthaman.

But isn't war supposed to be nameless?

Yes, as long as war is fought in the cosy studios of TV channels, it remains nameless and faceless. Those anchors who were/are baying for war as a weapon of revenge had clearly confused it with an India-Pakistan cricket match. Wars are not cricket matches. Cricket matches can be won, wars are never won. No one wins a war, not even the winner. The immorality of justifying a war lies in the fact that it cannot be won.

Imagine this, if we are so disturbed by one Abhinandan, what will happen if we are to go to war with Pakistan? Even in the most likely win-win situation we will still have a few hundred if not a thousand names and faces which will stick to our consciousness. With hands across your chests, how many of you remember Maninder Singh Attri, Sanjay Kumar Sinha, or Pradeep Singh? Well, these were the three martyrs among those 40 CRPF jawans killed in Pulwama some weeks ago. These are names and faces from a conflict which though have not slipped out of our memories but are actually lost into a din of numbers—three among 'those' forty. We are unified in our revenge for those forty but we fail to recognize them through names or faces because in our call for revenge and war, there are no names, there are no faces. How wrong is that? Rather how cruel, because wars do have names and faces, thousands of names and faces. Wars are about people, about their lives and unfortunately about their deaths.

Experiences from the Second World War have revealed that orgasms of jingoism should never be escalated to a level where war becomes inevitable. It required only a single man's xenophobic ideology of hate and segregation to throw the world into the mayhem of the Second World War. Ironically he too was supported by the media of his times. Wars are unfortunately fought by those who have no command over the very announcement of war. Political dispensations manufacture war for their benefit and then the onus of jingoism is laid on the shoulders of the poor soldier who fights this war.

The iron man of Germany, Otto von Bismarck had once said, anyone who has ever looked into the glazed eyes of a soldier dying on a battlefield will think hard before starting a war. His simple words are the best argumentative antidote for those who are calling for a war from their cosy studio chairs. There is one more wise word from Bismarck which needs to be mentioned here. He said, "people never lie so much as after a hunt, during a war or before an election."

(Earlier published at *The Wire*, March 2, 2019)

43

In Defence of My University

The single most dangerous preposition of fascists is persistence. Persistence with brutality and hate form the lynchpin of their efforts to control the masses. The disproportionate logic of hate cannot work unless it is hammered day in and day out like the blows of an ironsmith shaping a hot iron rod into an ugly sabre. Unfortunately in this new India, in the last four and a half years a disproportionate logic of hate has been flowing unabated through the screens of our TVs and the pages of our newspapers. The sabre has been in the making.

The alleged mishandling of the staff of a so-called 'nationalist' TV channel in the Aligarh Muslim University (AMU) campus and subsequent booking of 14 students on charges of sedition, is a classic example of this persistent brutality. We are told by hyperventilating TV anchors that AMU is a hub of terrorists and anti-nationals. Haven't we heard this before? The modus operandi is too simple and too comprehensible than when it was used nefariously for the first time on the campus of the Jawaharlal Nehru University (JNU) in the spring of 2016. The intent to create mischief at the AMU campus is not a new fable. In the last four and a half years there have been multiple attempts at maligning the university through vile campaigns. Whether it is the photograph of Jinnah (decorating a wall in the students' union hall) or the absolutely baseless news of non-availability of food to non-Muslim students during the month of Ramzan, AMU has been at the heart of the most potent anti-minority campaign seen in post-independent India.

Being an alumnus of the Aligarh Muslim University for a good ten years, I am privy to the life on the campus, and hence feel it appropriate to make a few points. To begin, by no stretch of imagination can the AMU campus be considered to be a heaven of liberal thought or free will. No, it isn't a JNU. Having said this, it is also not a madrasa training its students in the tenets of Islam. The AMU is as liberal or as radical, as patriarchal or as feminist, as conservative or as modern as any other university of the country. A quick glance at available data reveals that the representation of women teachers, proportion of female students, the number of research papers published, student placements, notable alumni and other such parameters of educational achievement in AMU are either the same or better than a large number of other central or state universities. Some of you might point out that I have left out the 'number of Muslim students enrolled' at AMU, as a measure of its so-called obscurantist thought. Yes, a rough estimate tells us that around sixty to sixty-five per cent students enrolled in AMU are Muslims. Should that not be a reason enough to worry in a nation, the present political dispensation of which is imagining to convert it into a Hindu rashtra?

Doing some arithmetic should explain this trend. The population of Muslims in India is 172 million or about 14.2 per cent of the total population of the country. The representation of Muslims in most educational Institutions is dismal. According to government figures, only 13.4 per cent of the total Muslims opt for higher education and only 4.8 per cent are graduate Muslims. With such a gloomy state of affairs, AMU becomes a suction point for a large number of young Muslim students. We may call this phenomena "educational ghettoization." This ghettoization is multi-factorial, working both on merit and favour as in any other similar educational institution of the country. The emergence of AMU as an educational ghetto for Muslims is not only a matter of worry for the Muslims alone but actually a matter of shame for the Indian society as a whole. Ghettoization in any form is a collective failure of the society.

What compels the Muslims to choose AMU as their alma mater? The factors which occur to me are probably the same as those which operate when a Muslim couple is denied a rental house in the country's prominent metropolises. I know some among you will be rolling your eyes and raising your eyebrows on my analogy but the fact remains that ghettoization whether in a neighbourhood or in education operates in the presence of bias and prejudice. Despicable campaigns of collective hatred against Muslims in the last four and a half years have only fortified this phenomena of ghettoization. It may thus be clarified that murderous attacks of cow vigilantes are not merely meant to end cow slaughter, it operates on a broader leash of instilling fear in the minds of the Muslims thereby further limiting their outreach whether in housing, education, or other aspects of social and political life. This unfortunately is the victory of the fascists.

So what should the student community of AMU do in these testing times?

They need to show restraint and patience. It is essential that they see through the programme of channels like the one in question and throttle their efforts of provocation. This, in my opinion, would be the greatest frustration for the fascist brigade. Equally important for the students is to keep getting stirred up with injustices around them. The World over, the most strong resistance to fascism and authoritarianism has come through institutes of higher learning. The students of AMU have a golden opportunity to align with similar cohorts at JNU, Jadhavpur University, Hyderabad University, Allahabad University, Madras University and all other educational institutes of learning which have seen an unprecedented assault on their values of freedom, liberty and free will. To be relevant in the times of authoritarianism it is essential that we remember what Paulo Freire, the greatest educationist of our times has once said, "education either functions as an instrument which is used to facilitate integration of the younger generation into the logic of the present system, and bring about conformity or it becomes the practice of freedom, the means by which men and women deal critically and creatively with reality and discover how to participate in the transformation of their world."

(Earlier published in the *The Wire*, February 14, 2019)

SECTION VI

HEALTHCARE AND ETHICS

44

A Low Priority Called Health

Ratna Devi and her nine-year-old daughter Seema (names changed) came to AIIMS, New Delhi. There was a large tumour on Seema's knee. It had been thriving on the little girl for a year. The family was from Rajasthan, around 400 kilometres from Delhi. The father was a farmer who owned a small piece of land, barely enough to sustain a family of six.

The tumour was treated initially at a private hospital in Jaipur, which prolonged the treatment, bleeding the family white. After it was found that the tumour was inoperable, Seema was sent to AIIMS with a small piece of paper that noted, "referred to a higher centre".

The initial treatment of the tumour cost the family Rs. 20,000 that was borrowed from the village moneylender at exorbitant interest. This now threatened the family's only piece of sustenance—the small patch of land. Seema's treatment in Delhi necessitated that the land be sold off.

The girl's limb was amputated at AIIMS and she was advised chemotherapy. But the family was not able to sustain living in Delhi, so Seema could not go through the complete process of chemotherapy. Without chemotherapy, I am sure, Seema would not have made it beyond one season. The hospital records showed that Seema was lost to follow-up. For me, she was murdered.

Seema's story is not a one-off in this country. An article published in *The Lancet* on June 26 reveals the tragedy of India's healthcare system in more objective terms. It evaluates the role of private players in the healthcare system of countries. The article brackets India with Nigeria in the group of nations with a "dominant private sector". At the time of our "tryst with destiny," we were made to believe that India was committing itself to socialist principles of governance. What went wrong that private players are predominant in the country's healthcare sector? Or was it that healthcare was purposefully left "unattended" so that private enterprise could run amok? Or perhaps, healthcare as a vital investment was—and is—beyond the imagination of the country's rulers?

The Lancet article slots Sri Lanka (along with Thailand) in a group where the "private sector complements the universalist public sector". The private sector's share in healthcare in India is an astonishing 78 per cent in urban areas and 71 per cent in rural areas; in Sri Lanka the share of the two sectors is nearly equal. What is more chilling is that public-funded healthcare insurance schemes in India, like the Rashtriya Swasth Beema Yojana, give more than 80 per cent of their reimbursements to the private sector. Simply put, money from public coffers is finding its way to private lockers through legitimate systems.

Poverty caused by expenditure on health has doubled in India in the past 15 years. Out-of-pocket health expenditure in India accounted for 6.8 per cent of household resources (and 12.1 per cent of non-food expenditure) in 2011-12. It does not need rocket science to understand that health is a vital resource for a nation. Healthy people contribute physically and intellectually to a nation's well-being. Unfortunately, however, health ranks low in the priorities of our rulers. At 1.3 per cent of the GDP, public spending on healthcare in India is lower than some of the poorest countries of the world. Bhutan and Ethiopia spend more on health than we do.

The UN Population Division's World Population Prospects reveals that Bangladesh has a better infant mortality (IMR) rate than India—31 versus 38 per 1,000 live births. Nepal's IMR is even better—29 per 1,000 life births—while Sri Lanka's IMR is better than a number of Western countries—eight per 1,000 live births. The fact that even war-ravaged Iraq has an

IMR of 27 per 1,000 live births speaks volumes of the shambles in which the Indian healthcare system finds itself.

The strengthening of private healthcare at the cost of the public sector has had disastrous consequences. Seema's story is that of every poor Indian family which is forced to look towards the private sector in the absence of a robust public health system. In a country like ours, where caste and economic stratification play vital roles, the public sector should be dominant in healthcare delivery. But private health providers have usurped what was a wonderful healthcare delivery infrastructure, on paper.

Increase in spending on healthcare, formulating relevant health policies (in a country where deaths due to diarrhoea are more than deaths due to SARS) and making the healthcare system accountable are some of the urgent necessities. But private health providers are here to stay.

Whether we let them thrive at our cost or make them realize that they need to complement and not surrogate the public health care system is a choice we need to make urgently.

(Earlier published as an OpEd in *The Indian Express*,
September 30, 2016)

45

Demonetization: Stories of Flesh and Blood

Beyond the orgasms of patriotism and far from the rhetoric of nationalism breathes the real India, an India of flesh and blood. And no matter what amount of chest thumping some among us do, it is getting clearer by the day that it was this real India which bled white following the demonetization drive announced by the government on November 8, 2016. And it wasn't about ATMs or Banks or GDP, or the growth rates, it was about people. No wonder, stories of real India are the ones, which are so full of blood and flesh.

Krishna (name changed) was supposed to bring his six-year old to us from a remote village near Jhansi for an imminent life and limb saving surgery. The little one had cancer of the thigh bone. She had finished chemotherapy and was due for surgery. Demonetization delayed the sowing of Krishna's crops, which in turn delayed his and his daughter's return to Delhi. A previous study by us had shown that every one week delay of surgery after chemotherapy in bone cancers, increased the risk of disease coming back by two folds. We operated on Krishna's daughter after a delay of two months. The family was happy, we were not, realizing very well what would happen in months to come!

By all standards Krishna's six-year-old was lucky. Priya (name changed) with a similar diagnosis, a twelve-year-old from Balaghat (Madhya Pradesh), could not make it at all to Delhi. Her father, a daily wage labourer, did all his calculations with the available funds and decided against coming for surgery. In the absence of work due to a cash crunch, a prospective trip to Delhi for further treatment with us would have put him and his four other children into jeopardy. I called him the other day; he apologized in the most sombre manner and told me that though Priya's tumour has grown big, her pain is less. She was happy to be in the company of her siblings. He had reconciled to fate! On coaxing to come, he disconnected, never to take our call again as if we didn't exist.

Aslam (name changed) the twenty-year-old tall man from a village in Moradabad had been waiting for surgery on a deformed leg. He had never walked straight and was alive to live this dream. We did a bit of geometry on his x rays and decided to give him a chance to walk again though there would be a cost of the implants used for this surgery. He willingly agreed, and borrowed a sum of Rs. 30,000 from the village moneylender. The money was given to him in the afternoon of November 8th and by the end of that day Aslam's dream and his money, had been reduced to dust. He now works to pay off his loan. He says surgery can happen in future; a future which now appears to have been swallowed by darkness.

I don't know if demonetization will be useful to purge out black money from the veins of India but I am sure that demonetization has tried to purge the poor India. As a nation we have yet again failed the common, poor Indian. Nations are not about boundaries and maps, or about mighty Himalayas and the vast Thar. Neither is it about a tricolour or an anthem. Nations are about beating hearts and warm breaths; of dreams and hopes, of a common future. Nations can never be more important than its people, never. Nations don't make us, we make a nation. And what use would a nation be to the likes of Krishna, Priya or Aslam if it bled them to death in the name of cleansing its economy? Why is the greater good of a nation always on the corpses of the poor? Why the hell do the poor not filter through into the impervious imagination of our rulers? It evades my thought.

(Earlier published at *Countercurrents.org*, December 18, 2016)

46

Cash and Care

More than a month after the government announced its demonetization drive, the country has begun to realize its social, economic and political implications. As we know, the move has affected processes and practices that require cash transactions throughout the country. It will take some time for the full impact of the demonetization process to manifest but its short-term implications are already visible. These need careful evaluation. One does not need rocket science to understand that one area where the cash crunch has affected the common people, directly, is access to healthcare.

Working in the country's largest public health hospital, I have realized that demonetization has hit healthcare access in a significant way. There have been requests to postpone surgeries, patients have dropped out from follow-up clinics and a significant number of appointments have been cancelled. The AIIMS's orthopaedic outpatient department (OPD) saw a 22 per cent dip in patients in November (between November 11 and December 2) as compared to October 2016 (between October 4 and October 30). National festivals, inclement weather and school holidays usually cause a dip in patient attendance at the AIIMS but none of these reasons were at work during this period.

In India's three-tier healthcare delivery system, people have to travel to access healthcare. A significant number of patients who consult doctors at the AIIMS are from outside Delhi. Demonetization has severely hit people's capacity to move out of their hometowns to seek health advice even though public funding systems are, to a significant extent, taking care of the costs of medicines, surgery, and implants.

The Indian Council on Competitiveness' roundtable on healthcare has identified financial barrier as the toughest obstacle in the way of common people accessing healthcare. Demonetization and lack of funds have, unfortunately, aggravated matters. The corridors of hospitals like the AIIMS are full of stories on credit spending, particularly by people facing dire situations, including those suffering from diseases such as cancer. Many patients say the fund crunch has forced them to take credits. This aggravates poverty caused by healthcare expenditure.

At the AIIMS, there is practically no demand on the patient's pocket. Even then, there has been a significant reduction in patient numbers. We can imagine what the cash crunch has done to patients seeking private healthcare. In a country where the private sector delivers around 78 per cent of healthcare, the situation arising out of demonetization can be anybody's guess. My friends who work in private medical institutions relate similar experiences: Patient attendance has gone down, surgeries are being postponed and people are resorting to credit. So even when the full impact of demonetization is yet to unfurl, common people appear to be cutting down on healthcare costs. This is a serious challenge and needs active government intervention. It is difficult for the medical fraternity to give a clear solution because the problem lies in bringing the patient to the hospital and not initiating actual treatment. And this problem stems from the absence of cash in hand.

A robust government health insurance policy (with a home to hospital coverage) would have gone a long way in mitigating this situation. Measures like provision of cash at hospital kiosks and registration counters, free transport services for patients and educating the masses to avoid cost-cutting on healthcare could have prevented people from (forcefully) opting out of medical treatment.

We are told to be patient (and rightly so) during this process of massive transformation of the Indian economy. Unfortunately, however, preaching patience to the ill, disabled and the dying can be tricky. Yes, we need to cleanse the system but that should not be at the cost of the poor who are dependent on cash for essential needs like healthcare. Doing so is unethical and dangerous.

(Earlier published as an OpEd in
The Indian Express, December 16, 2016)

47

Clinical Trials in India Need Better Regulations

On May 20, 2017, the Drug Controller General of India (DCGI), G.N. Singh, addressing the annual US-India BioPharma and Healthcare Summit in Boston, announced that the government is set to launch a new clinical trials policy that will promise greater transparency and better checks for patient safety.

A new clinical trials policy is long awaited. Hence, it is imperative that a clear understanding of the pros and cons of clinical trials be brought into the public domain vis-à-vis a resource challenged healthcare environment like ours.

Clinical trials are the cornerstone of evidence-based medicine. With a huge population and an easy access to a wide variety of treatment of native diseases, India forms a hotbed for clinical trials for both national and international researchers. India is a signatory to the World Trade Organization (WTO). As a signatory country, it became fully compliant to the Trade Related Intellectual Property Rights (TRIPS) in January 2005. Thus, between 2005 and 2009, clinical trials sprung out like wild weeds throughout the length and breadth of the country. There was an overwhelming torrent of Contract Research Organizations (CRO) or the sponsors of such trials.

During the peak of clinical trials in India, it was revealed (in 2009) that 24,000 girls were enrolled in the Human Papilloma Virus (HPV) vaccination trial which, when investigated, was found to have irregularities in informed consent, a key component of all clinical trials. It is believed that between 2005 and 2012, about 2,800 patients have died across the country while participating in all clinical trials conducted by pharmaceutical companies. In fact, there has been extreme scepticism around the conduct and results of clinical trials in countries like India and China.

In a study published in the *Journal of Clinical Epidemiology* in January 2011, it was concluded that reporting of trials in Indian and Chinese journals falls short in quality when compared to trials published in Western journals. Through an active role of the highest court of the country and concerted efforts of health activists, the HPV trial in India was not only halted but a national debate ensued on the conduct of clinical trials in general. It raised some important ethical questions on the feasibility of conducting clinical trials in India. As the government prepares to modify the clinical trial policy of the country, it is essential that the subject be revisited and debated to ensure the efficacy and safety of clinical trials in India, not only from an ethical, but from all points of view. The patient is the single most important component of a clinical trial and all efforts should be made to safeguard the interests of the patient.

Most, if not all, clinical trials happen because of financial interests of the pharmaceutical or implant company/CRO involved in the trial. To clearly understand the pecuniary involvements of the CRO in question, it is crucial that the government should ask for further transparency in such trials. In this respect, Phase 4 clinical trials (post-marketing trials) are the most important as many Phase 4 trials are meant to lure doctors into increasing the number of patients using the said drug/implant/treatment. Thus, the conduct of Phase 4 trials need to be specially monitored and regulated by the concerned governmental body. The revisions in the clinical trials policy should have a more humanitarian perspective besides the regular cliché of scientific advancement as is pushed forth by the researcher and/or CRO. Regulations of financial disclosures need to be strengthened and the onus of such disclosures should be on the CRO or the investigator.

It is shameful that India harbours a significant quantum of major illnesses that are not seen in other parts of the world. In the recent Global Burden of Disease study published in *The Lancet*, India ranked 154th out of 195 countries as far as access to healthcare and quality are concerned. Despite there being numerous patients with varied conditions in the country, most clinical trials, unfortunately, still focus on ailments that have a Western bias to their origin or numbers. The number of trials on indigenous innovative methodologies in the diagnosis, treatment and surveillance of diseases typical to the Indian subcontinent are very few. Most of such indigenous trials are either poorly conceived and hence dropped at the evaluation stage or are copies of ongoing trials in some other parts of the world. This needs to be changed and incentives should be given to trials and researchers working on indigenous conditions or those testing innovations in the treatment methodology meant for conditions typically seen in India. Incentives should not mean "ease of approval" of such trials. Having said this, such incentives can be a double-edged sword and the government should be meticulous in evaluating which clinical trial can be called indigenous or innovative. Accredited higher technology centres should only be allowed to do such trials.

Following the disaster of 2009 (HPV vaccinations), it was realized that the compensation to trial subjects was an important area which needed a change. The interests of the patient are sacred in a clinical trial. It is imperative that the state ensures that the concerned CRO should bear all responsibility of harm to a patient during such trials. This can even be extended to criminal liability in such cases. Developing a clinical trial insurance scheme and making it mandatory for all CROs/ investigators to implement the same will be a right step in this regard. In fact, it would be good if the government can consider the track record of the sponsoring company/CRO conducting the trial. Premium rates for such an insurance can be decided by various local factors of the trial including the stage of the trial, expected or actual trial outcomes, drug/implant being tested and the speculated extent of harm by the drug/treatment/intervention. Besides compensations in the event of harm, the government should consider fixing a minimum payment of honorarium to all participants of a clinical trial in India. It may also be notified through appropriate legislatures that drugs/implants/treatments arising out of clinical trials conducted in India should be provided at adequately discounted rates or for free in the country. If a country's citizens are used for trials, it becomes their first right to get the tested material on a heavily discounted rate. Not doing so paints a picture of people being used as guinea pigs.

Clinical trials are here to stay. It is important that such trials are better regulated with the patient or the subject at the centre stage of all policy considerations in this respect. Safeguarding the interests of the patient in a clinical trial is as holy as the grail. Scientific advancement and patient safety are two sides of the same coin. We must realize that we cannot have one at the cost of the other. Adequate regulations which safeguard patients' interests and ease the conduct of clinical trials will go a long way in establishing a "culture" of clinical trials in this country.

(Earlier published in *The Wire*, June 22, 2017)

48

India's Healthcare System is Suffering from a Crisis of Compassion

Every year, July 1 is celebrated as Doctors' Day across India. In the last few months, there has been unprecedented violence against doctors leading to strikes and agitations in many parts of the country, so let us try and see if we can decipher the recent events through a historical perspective.

Sir Joseph W. Bhore was the Chairman of the Health Survey and Development Committee—formed by the colonial rulers of India in 1943 with an aim to evaluate the then existing health conditions and health set up in the country, and give recommendations for the future. Dorothy Porter, in her immensely useful book *The History of Public Health and the Modern State*, described the formation of this committee as a 'crisis of legitimation' by the British rulers, as after the end of the Second World War, there was significant failure of health services across the country.

The committee submitted its recommendation in three volumes in 1946, a year before independence. It severely criticized the health status in British India and brought to light the dramatic comparisons between the values of important health statistics (like infant mortality and life expectancy) in England (and Wales) and in India. Most of the recommendations of the Bhore Committee had a preventive narrative but there was an emphasis on the integration of preventive and therapeutic services at all levels.

In one of its most far-reaching verdicts, the Bhore Committee had borrowed the words of the famous Swiss medical historian, Prof. Henry E. Sigerist, to say that the doctor should be a 'social physician protecting and guiding the people'. To me, this was the soul of the numerous recommendations of the committee as it had more to do with the individual member of the healthcare delivery system rather than a means to run the administrative machinery of healthcare.

Even 70 years after it was recommended, the Indian doctor is yet to take over the mantle of a social physician and a leader protecting and guiding the people. In fact, the medical fraternity has hardly ever attempted to take this role seriously in postcolonial India, barring a few exceptions. Is that a lack of will of the Indian doctor or a lack of understanding of the basic tenets of socialistic parlance within the realms of Indian society which led to this failure, is debatable.

I will not be wrong in concluding that medical students in India are kept away from this aspect of training where they can be sensitized to the needs of the poor, the underprivileged and the downtrodden of society—the sections which are most in need of a 'social physician' and a leader. The three months of rural posting (after MBBS) which was started following the recommendations of the Bhore Committee with this very objective, is too limited and inconsequential in evoking any sense of understanding in the minds of these budding doctors to take over as social physicians and community leaders.

The materialistic lure, better job opportunities and poor understanding of the operational complexities of Indian society, are some of the causes which prevent the development of 'social physicians' from amongst this group. It may be argued that to be a social physician as recommended by Bhore, it is not necessary to be only practising in the rural hinterlands of the country and rightly so. The 'social physician leader' can evolve anywhere. It is not the place of practice for a doctor that makes him/her a leader but rather a sense of compassion towards the subjects he/she is bound to take care of—an understanding of the fact that the *diseased* are always more important than the *disease*.

In a country that sees more than 1,500-2,000 trained doctors migrate to foreign soils every year, how do we arouse compassion and train them to fit into the role of a 'social physician' is the question, which unfortunately does not have a clear-cut answer. So from a 'crisis of legitimization' at the time of inception of the Bhore Committee, we have landed into a 'crisis of compassion' in the present day.

Having said this, despite a reluctance of the Indian medical fraternity to serve its own people with the zest of a social activist, there are examples from India itself where doctors have taken over the role suggested by Bhore and his committee. People like Dr. Binayak Sen, Dr. Abhay Bang and Dr. Rani Bang, Dr. Arun Gadre, the doctors at the Jan Swasthya Sahyog and Dr. Abhay Shukla are some of the names I can recollect from the present generation. These are individuals who have gone beyond the precincts of conventional thinking and action and have taken up healthcare not only as a means of preventing and treating disease but also as a weapon to fight for the rights of the weaker sections of society, train them to stand for their cause and thus emerge as leaders for large segments of the Indian populace.

The practice of medicine gives an opportunity of changing society from within. So on this Doctors' Day, India's medical professionals should realize that beyond the lures of the pharmaceutical industry and tons of capital, lies an unexplored horizon of hope. To evolve as social physicians of Bhore, along with the science of healing, we need to learn the art of compassion. According to Hippocrates, the father of medicine, wherever the art of medicine is loved, there is also a love of humanity.

(Earlier published in *The Wire*, July 1, 2017)

49

Unless Morality and Medicine Combine, Regulating Private Medical Establishments is a Must

Bob Dylan, the Nobel Prize winner for literature 2017, wrote a popular song following the death of boxer Davey Moore in a fight. It was called 'Who Killed Davey Moore'. The wordings of the song are significant:

Who killed Davey Moore
Why an' what's the reason for?
"Not me," says the gambling man
With his ticket stub still in his hand
"It wasn't me that knocked him down
My hands never touched him none
I didn't commit no ugly sin
Anyway, I put money on him to win
It wasn't me that made him fall
No, you can't blame me at all"

Pradipto Dasa (name changed), an average shopkeeper from the Kalibarhi area of Kolkata, came to us last year with a nagging knee pain which was treated in at least three different private hospitals in his city without much relief. Two of these three hospitals have a big name in Kolkata. He had undergone two key hole surgeries and one open surgery, only to be told that there was nothing wrong. The total expenditure incurred for knowing that "nothing" was wrong was close to Rs 2.5 lakhs.

The young man harboured a benign tumour around the

knee, which was completely missed by all three surgeons. It was easily cured by us with a simple, one-time surgery. Last week, he returned for a routine follow-up and told me that he was very happy to know that 'Didi' has tightened the screws against private hospitals in the state. He was vindicated for his missed tumour, he thought.

Mamata Banerjee, the Chief Minister of West Bengal, has introduced a new legislation called the West Bengal Clinical Establishments (Registration, Regulation and Transparency) Act, 2017, to regulate the working of private clinical establishments in the state. The said Act has been brought in after repealing the (existing) Act of 2010. The provisions in Banerjee's version of the Act call for stringent action against hospitals which stray from patient care. The Act has led to the creation of the West Bengal Clinical Establishment Regulatory Commission (WBCERC), which is a watchdog that will take care of hospitals not towing the ethical line.

The new legislation is already drawing flak from multiple corners, but mainly from private clinical establishments. Professional acquaintances and friends in Kolkata reveal that the medical fraternity is split down the middle, with equal support for and disapproval of the Act. Those who support the Act feel that there is an unfair attempt to paint the Act as being against doctors. According to them, the spirit of the Clinical Establishment Act of West Bengal is not against doctors per se, but against private clinical establishments only. Of course it will help in apprehending erring doctors, but it does not, in its provisions, specify methods to take direct action against doctors. The other group agrees with the fact that the Act is not directly against doctors, but the onus of an act of commission or omission will finally rest at the doorstep of the doctor. They feel that hospitals, in cases of neglect, will nonchalantly wash their hands, leaving the doctors to face the music. Both sides of this divide have a valid point which needs to be seen in a broader context.

Why Was This Act Necessary?

There isn't an easier question to answer. We live in an extremely greedy neoliberal world, where everything and anything is up for sale. Healthcare too has not remained untouched by this unwavering attempt to capture wealth. The takeover of healthcare by private players (including big corporate groups) in India is nearly complete, with more than 78 per cent of healthcare being delivered through the private system. Since so much of the healthcare sector is controlled by private enterprises, it is only imperative that the system will develop amoral flaws and hence need regulation. And there we see the need for an Act like the one introduced by the West Bengal government.

It will not be wrong to conclude that the gradual dwindling of influence of the Medical Council of India (MCI) over the last decade or so has further necessitated the inception of such Acts. Embezzlement within the MCI by its past president(s) and other officials (some of whom were chargesheeted by the courts) is one of the worst tragedies in Indian medical practice. Not surprisingly, the muck within the MCI was so deep that the highest court had to intervene, undermining the role of an ethical body which is supposed to give "certificates of good standing" to its own doctors. The MCI, unlike its counterpart the General Medical Council (GMC) of the United Kingdom, has failed both in safeguarding the interests of its patients and in regulating doctors. There have been instances when the GMC has issued warnings to doctors for driving cars without proper insurance, as this is unbecoming of a responsible doctor. Compare that to the MCI, which has a very passive role in monitoring acts of medical neglect which appear now and then in the national media.

Having said this, the West Bengal (state) MCI still retains the power to act against doctors, as all complaints pertaining to medical impropriety will still be addressed to the state MCI either directly by the complainant or by the WBCERC.

I suppose Indian doctors and the Indian healthcare delivery

system (both private and public) have committed enough faults in patient care to warrant the need for a more stringent body to look into the mess. The devil has been let loose for too long and Acts like the one in West Bengal are inevitable. What is surprising is that other state governments have not regulated medical practice through similar Acts, more so in the absence of a potent MCI. It is, therefore, wrong on the part of the medical fraternity to say that they are being targeted. They become targets in this kind of manner only because they are accountable to the people of this land, not by the virtue of an authoritative diktat but by their own misdeeds in patient care.

Doctors' Concerns

However, doctors' concerns vis-à-vis the West Bengal Clinical Establishments (Registration, Regulation and Transparency) Act, 2017 are not without valid reasons. In big clinical establishments, say corporate hospitals, the doctors are only a small part of the money-making machinery. Most of these hospitals are run like profit-making businesses, with administrative controls on the doctors. To expect that such a hospital will take measures to safeguard the interests of its own doctors is laughable. The main aim of such a venal set up would be to put the onus of an error squarely on the doorstep of the doctor, jeopardizing his/her career and hampering accountability and justice. It is thus essential to build checks and balances within the Clinical Establishment Act, so that such hospitals do not get away with passing the buck to the doctor. With a good and distinguished panel of healthcare professionals (and not only bureaucrats) on the administrative bodies of the commission, such misappropriation can be taken care of.

A large part (in fact a majority) of clinical establishments in India are not run by corporate enterprises. They are run by individuals or a small group of doctors. Acts like the one in question are going to affect these hospitals (the so-called nursing homes) most profoundly. The owners of these clinical establishments seem to be the most perturbed by the establishment of the WBCERC. To be worried about accountability is often proof enough of dishonesty. The owners of such medical establishments need not be disquieted. There is a very simple way to get around this Act: Practise medicine with ethics. Stick to the tenets of the Hippocratic Oath and practise the art of medicine without fear or favour.

Like in Bob Dylan's 'Who Killed Davey Moore', the crime must be owned up to. The onus of patient neglect cannot and should not be ignored. We, as doctors, have let the devil loose for too long. Immanuel Kant's moralistic ethics of medical practice need to be retaught to the next generation of doctors, so that Acts like the one in question are not needed at all. But till that dawn breaks, there is no doubt that we need administrative and legal checks on doctors.

(Earlier published in *The Wire*, August 22, 2017)

50

Not at the Click of a Mouse

In his Independence Day address Prime Minister Narendra Modi talked about the digitization of AIIMS, the country's largest public hospital. He said, "when people used to come to AIIMS, they had to wait for two to three days to just know when they will have to undergo tests. We have been able to change that system. There is provision for online registration and seeking online appointment with doctors. A patient's medical records are available online. We want to develop this culture throughout the country with respect to healthcare systems." As an AIIMS employee for the past 13 years, I must say that digitization has changed things. But unfortunately the picture is not as rosy as described by the Prime Minister.

Digitization has meant extra waiting time for patients coming from outside Delhi. Most emails and phone calls seeking appointments are from people from the upper strata of society. Email access or access to a physician's contact number is restricted to those who can read and write and have access to a computer or a mobile phone. Digitization of the process of outpatient appointments threatens to restrict the common person's accessibility to healthcare.

The digital appointment system at AIIMS was launched in July 2015. As part of the "transformation" drive at AIIMS, the institute's security was beefed up, various outpatient gates were designated and patients could seek appointments online or on the phone. It thus became almost impossible for patients to physically approach doctors without prior appointments, for which there were long waiting periods. So some may ask how is this different from the past? In the past too, AIIMS's outpatient departments were flooded with patients and the waiting times were equally long. But in those days, the human element prevailed and patients found their way to consultation chambers as a result of the courtesy of kind paramedics, nurses and onsite staff (I agree there was a risk of corrupt practices but these risks persist even with online procedures).

On questioning an enthusiastic employee of the Tata Consultancy Services (TCS), which is among the agencies involved in the digitization of AIIMS's OPD appointment system, I was told that the measure was part of a "crowd management" policy. Crowd management? I was reminded of Delhi police constables controlling protesting crowds at Delhi's Jantar Mantar. TCS, it appears, is confused between transforming the country's passport issuing service (a task it has, undoubtedly, performed well) and transforming the nation's largest and busiest public hospital which deals with the sick and the dying.

It could be argued, in favour of the digital appointment process, that we cannot let the "human element" delay the process of digitization—an essential requirement for any modern-day healthcare system. Yes, we shouldn't but in a country like India where poverty, illiteracy and caste play significant roles in how people access healthcare services it would be imprudent to ignore the importance of a thinking person mediating between the patient and the physician. It is impossible to imagine that digitization alone can bring a patient to a tertiary healthcare centre, particularly because we lack a robust referral system. A referral service would have been far better and a useful "gate-keeping" instrument than actually restricting patients in the name of crowd management.

The problems of an one-size-fits-all implementation strategy for online patient registration and clinic appointments in an underdeveloped country—and in developed countries as well—are well known. A study from China revealed that around 90 per cent patients showed reluctance in adopting an online appointment system. The reasons for their reluctance included lack of access to the internet, low computer skills and incompatibility of the online appointment service with patient requirements. I am sure such factors hobble the online appointment system in India as well.

Undoubtedly that digitization leads to transparency, ensures patient follow-up and improves healthcare delivery but the perils of hastily digitizing a hospital like AIIMS, which caters to the poor and illiterate, should have been obvious to the policymakers. Healthcare systems should be digitized in a slow and inclusive manner. There should be flexibility in procedures to ensure that patients are not sacrificed at the altar of crowd management. Strengthening the prevailing peripheral healthcare set-ups and linking them to tertiary centres like AIIMS will ensure a better referral system. Technology does play an important role in the delivery of healthcare, but not to be aware of ground realities in the country is the worst misuse of technology.

(Earlier published as an OpEd in *The Indian Express*, November 15, 2016)

51

How Not to Treat Tuberculosis

Last month, the Delhi High Court acceded to the plea of an 18-year-old girl that she be given access to Bedaquiline, an anti-TB drug found useful in treating multi-drug or extensively drug resistant disease (abbreviated as MDR/XDR TB). The girl had to move court because Bedaquiline was recently added in the armamentarium of the Revised National Tuberculosis Control Programme of India (RNTC) with significant riders. Since Bedaquiline was the first major anti-TB drug discovered in the last 40 years, the government restricted its use for fear of TB mycobacterium developing resistance to the medicine. Since February 2016, its availability is restricted to just six hospitals in five different cities (Delhi, Mumbai, Ahmedabad, Chennai and Guwahati). The complainant resided in Patna; her domicile status was held against her from being treated with Bedaquiline.

In a country which has an annual incidence of around 99,000 new cases of multi-drug resistant TB, only 164 patients have been enrolled for Bedaquiline therapy in these hospitals till date. Clearly, there is something amiss in the government's policy in rolling out Bedaquiline for XDR and MDR tuberculosis. The rationing of Bedaquiline by the government on the fears of drug resistance is understandable. The rampant use of anti-tubercular medicines has resulted in India having 4.80 lakh new cases of MDR TB in 2015. But is there a scientific rationale for rationing the drug, of putting it beyond the reach of the patient (and the health practitioner), to prevent the development of resistance against it?

Ever since Penicillin was discovered by Alexander Fleming in 1929, an "antibiotic revolution" has been ushered in medicine with new antibiotics flooding the market every year. But there is hardly any antibiotic against which "no resistance" has been reported. The only way in which antibiotic resistance can be prevented is not to use the antibiotic, which, of course, is not possible. Preventing resistance against Bedaquiline is a must, but the manner in which this is being done is impractical and undemocratic.

A community perspective on the use of Bedaquiline is a must in a resource-challenged country like India. In fact, a Joint TB Monitoring Mission in its report in 2015 pointed out the lacunae within the RNTC in the management of multi-drug-resistant cases. The high power committee suggested that the prime reason for the rise in drug-resistant TB is the inherent weakness of state-run TB control programmes and the lack of awareness among patients, who do not complete the recommended six-month medication. Besides, slashing the five-year budget of RNTC from Rs. 6,500 crore to Rs. 4,500 crore by the present government has only added to the problem of TB control in the country. Thus, it is thought-provoking whether it is fair to "punish" the patient by denying a drug, for the wrongdoings of a system and the state? Besides, scientific evidence suggests that a delay in the treatment of MDR/XDR cases of tuberculosis only makes the community more susceptible to the spread of infection by the multi-drug resistant TB organism. Studies on the use of drugs like Bedaquiline in the early stages of multi-drug resistant scenarios in South Africa showed better results both in terms of disease cure and in the restriction of community spread of the disease. It is thus imperative that the use of Bedaquiline early in the disease will have far better results than in denying its use through impractical statutes.

The issue of the geographical restriction of Bedaquiline may be one of its kind in this country. Restricting patients and means to treat them in specific regions is unprecedented. Other than preventing the development of resistance to the drug, I am not sure what other elements of scientific reasoning have gone into the government's decision to geographically restrict the distribution of Bedaquiline. If the priority is prevention of drug resistance, it could be attained by methods less draconian than controlling the availability of the drug. Strict surveillance of MDR/XDR cases, better community outreach programmes to educate the patient and the healthcare provider against treatment dropout, quality assurance on available anti-TB drugs and educating physicians against the irresponsible, injudicious use of anti-tubercular therapy are far better, though more difficult, means of preventing MDR/XDR. Restriction of treatment based on the geographical location of patients is the worst form of federal arrogance which a state can unleash on its citizens. Regional domiciles should not dilute the principles of equipoise in the eyes of the state. Some patients cannot be more equal than others.

TB is a disease of the poor. In his budget speech, the Finance Minister committed to the eradication of TB by 2025. A compassionate approach supplemented by scientific rationality is a must in promoting, not rationing, Bedaquiline therapy. Besides, the Delhi HC order should be an eye opener for policymakers to rethink means to roll out Bedaquiline more effectively and to introduce other drugs like Delaminate in the treatment of MDR/XDR TB in India.

(Earlier published as an OpEd in *The Indian Express*, February 11, 2017)

52

You Pay More, You Get More

Recently, the Finance Ministry has asked the All India Institute of Medical Sciences, New Delhi, to review its user charges, that is, money charged from patients for OPD registration, lab tests, room and bed rentals, etc. The institute administration has already convened a meeting to work on the logistics of the proposal. It was said that the user charges at AIIMS were last reviewed 20 years ago and since then, its expenditure has grown many fold. Therefore, it was essential to revise these charges—a clear indicator that revision implied an imminent increase in charges.

This recommendation stands to affect millions of poor Indians who look towards AIIMS as a last resort. Unfortunately, the model of development such measures promote is far from people-centric. In recent times, successive elected governments have acted more in favour of private players than in the interest of public enterprises. We have seen this "corporate connivance" of the state in many sectors, including education, roadways, telecom, even in health. The move is against welfare economics and should worry us as much as the proposed opening up of a separate registration counter at the AIIMS for "VIP" patients; a move that had to be scrapped in the face of faculty opposition.

In the absence of a universal, institutional arrangement to pay for patients' health needs (medical insurance, for example), low charges are the only respite for the poor. For an average Indian, it is not easy to reach a healthcare delivery point, more so in rural hinterlands. Besides quality, accessibility and affordability of healthcare, biases of gender, caste, illiteracy and economic deficiency play a pivotal role in healthcare delivery. Despite free treatment at government hospitals, more than 78 per cent of healthcare in India is through private players. It is therefore essential for policymakers to consider that those who do make it to a government healthcare provider are either exempted or minimally charged. This will facilitate the flow of patients to a government healthcare set-up like the AIIMS and will hopefully be a factor in reducing the patient "leak" into expensive private set-ups.

An elected government should promote its services (at least concerning health and education) among those who have elected it to power. This opens up government systems to critical appraisal, which in turn will lead to the betterment of these services. The propagandists of increasing user charges have a simple argument: You pay more, you get more. The issue is not so simple.

The world over, contribution of user charges towards improving the healthcare delivery system is negligible, if any. In fact, studies from India have shown that increasing user charges within the government healthcare set-up has reduced the utilization of the health services at least two-fold. From amongst all government healthcare set-ups in the country, the AIIMS enjoys the most stocky budget and an increase in user charges will only add a minuscule amount of profit while taking away a significant chunk of patients. This is no less than actual denial of tertiary, world-class healthcare services to the masses. Before levying higher user charges, the government should audit the utilization of resources (and money) to large hospitals like the AIIMS. It is possible that the amount unutilized might be equal to, or less than, the user charges it proposes to impose.

A more humane approach would be to further reduce/exempt user charges as has been shown in a number of studies from low and middle-income countries. Cutting subsidies to private enterprises like health insurers could be a way of preventing the extra burden on the end user. An actual increase in the annual health budget by the government will go a long way in preventing the burden of charges to be passed on to its citizens. The government should realize that prioritizing health within the country is the most important economic method to prevent disease and promote health.

(Earlier published in *The Indian Express*, March 11, 2017)

53

Cure Lies Elsewhere

At the inauguration of a hospital in Surat recently, Prime Minister Narendra Modi announced his government's intent to bring in a law whereby doctors will have to prescribe only generic medicines. Any conscientious citizen of the country, doctors included, will applaud this initiative as it intends to provide direct financial relief to the common man and limit the influence of major private companies in the pharmaceutical market. Unfortunately, the outcome of the initiative may turn out to be unhealthy in practice.

As with most policies, the devil is in the detail. In India, the unholy doctor-pharma nexus results in a symbiotic relationship leading to unnecessary, expensive prescriptions. This, of course, is a matter of grave concern. But it is important to realize that besides the doctor, this unholy nexus also has the pharmaceutical company as an equal partner. The intended legal proposal of the government has the means to rein in the doctor to an extent, but the pharmaceutical company goes unscathed. At present, these companies "bribe" doctors into writing drugs of their choice because doctors have the power to prescribe medicines. Once this power is taken away, as intended by the proposed law, the onus of giving the branded generic drug will be with the chemist. It does not require rocket science to understand where the pharmaceutical companies will focus then.

There is a chronic shortage of drug inspectors who look after quality control at manufacturing and dispensing sites of medicines. In 2010, 55 per cent posts of drug inspectors in

Maharashtra were lying vacant. In the absence of stringent controls over dispensing chemists in the country, the move will create havoc. Besides substituting prescribed drugs, chemists could be selling more expensive generic drugs to patients, thereby defeating the very purpose of the law. Quality is the other major issue with generic drugs. In the last few years, the US Food and Drug Administration (USFDA) has initiated action against many Indian pharmaceutical companies for alleged violation of good manufacturing practices and other irregularities at the drug manufacturing facilities. This happened mainly with generic drugs, which were manufactured in India and exported to the US. With such poor-quality controls in manufacturing, the intent of the legislation will be compromised.

It looks as if the government wants to work in reverse direction to cleanse the grimy Indian drug market. A logical step would have been to institute better quality control in the manufacture of generic drugs first, test their bioequivalence with standard branded medicines, build doctor and patient confidence on the product and then, push for a change in prescription behaviour of physicians. In fact, research papers from across the globe show that physicians need to be reassured and educated about the Drug Regulatory Authority approval system of generic medicines regarding their bioequivalence, quality, efficacy and safety to facilitate use.

The policy to implement legislation for the prescription of generic drugs by doctors is undoubtedly a good move. But the haste shown by the government in bringing this measure is odd and populist. It is extremely important to reduce the burden of health-related costs on common people, but instead of jumping the gun on generic medicines, alternative methods to reduce costs and improving quality of drugs should be given priority. Bringing in a National Medicine Pricing Policy would be a simple but very effective way in controlling drug prices, without taking away the choice of prescription from doctors. This could be easily done through the government's National

Pharmaceutical Pricing Authority. Prescription pattern monitoring rules need to be implemented stringently to dent the doctor-pharma nexus. Increasing drug manufacturing units and investing heavily in drug research and development will effectively make India "drug self-sufficient" with a wider and cost-effective "drug reach". Better control of branded generics and patent generics are also measures the government should work on. The government should realize that intent reveals desire, but action reveals commitment. Half-hearted action will only jeopardize future action.

(Earlier published in *The Indian Express*, May 12, 2017)

54

Dignity, But For Whom?

A five-judge bench of the Supreme Court of India has legalized passive euthanasia and permitted the "living will". A person making such a will can state that medical support be withdrawn when he or she becomes terminally ill. The verdict has been hailed for its far-reaching impact on Indian society. Though the five judges differed on the matter, they were unanimous in allowing "living will".

As a surgeon who has been treating bone cancers for the last 15 years, I have seen innumerable patients die and survive. I, therefore, have a different perspective on the judgment. I believe that death has an immorality of its own. It is inevitable. The Supreme Court judgment has, in a sense, added morality to death. Paul Kalanithi in his bestseller, *When Breath Becomes Air*, has written: "But knowing that even if I'm dying, until I actually die, I am still living." For physicians who see the dying from close quarters, nothing could be truer. The process of life is not over till it ends. Whether this judgment is bound to change that perception is something we will have to wait and see.

A living will which allows one to choose death is a privilege which only the educated can avail. In a country which is riddled with ignorance and illiteracy, who can make such a living will is no secret. Thus, in a sense, the provision of passive euthanasia in India becomes exclusive to the educated, if not the elite. The judgment draws blood from similar judgments and cases in the US and Australia. To believe that we can emulate the legal provisions of these nations on a contentious issue like euthanasia is not only difficult but outrageous. For many of us who treat terminally-sick patients, the judgment appears blemished as it bestows death (through passive euthanasia) upon some while "actively" denies it to others. A law that does not take into account the poverty and ignorance in society requires a serious re-think.

It is also important to realize that the spectrum of something as certain as a "terminal" illness or even a vegetative state is very broad. As physicians, we see patients come out of their terminal states to lead a normal life. To assume that this is uncommon is unaffordable frivolousness. The premise of using passive euthanasia in terminal conditions as allowed by the Supreme Court judgment can be easily misused by doctors, kin and even by patients. This is something that needs constant evaluation by the treating physician, free from the diktats of the law. A brief review of the healthcare services is a must before we accept the concept of passive euthanasia as interpreted by the Court. India's healthcare facilities are among the poorest in the world. Most of passive (and active) euthanasia across the globe is practised by hospice and palliative care specialists. The concept of hospice services (which are the end of life services within a medical or home setup) are practically non-existent in India. In the absence of well-organized hospice services in most government and private hospitals, there is no guarantee of a decent death to the patients who will choose passive euthanasia.

The judgment makes an interesting point: "It is to be borne in mind that passive euthanasia fundamentally connotes absence of any overt act either by the patient or by the doctors." This is interesting because it raises a question of morality versus legality on the part of the doctor who will preside over the death of a willing patient. Doctors are bound by acts of commission or omission which should be in tune with the patient's welfare. The intent of treatment is defined through our acts of omission or commission, which should help the patient to get better. For example, what should a doctor do in the case of a dying patient on a ventilator who had made a living will? According to the judgment, the doctor is not allowed to administer a lethal injection (active euthanasia). To slowly withdraw life support would mount to an act of commission thereby raising significant questions of morality and will be against the legal words of the honourable Court. This grey area leaves dangerous space for manipulation and even murder.

The argument on euthanasia is always on moral grounds—right versus wrong, murder versus suicide. Judgments like the one by the Supreme Court of India represent the traits of an evolving society. We are a complex society entrenched in our past and living in a promised future. For passive euthanasia to be seriously considered as an option in a country like ours, we need to keep in mind the words of Immanuel Kant, the proponent of the principles of ethics which form the basis of medical ethics. He argued that morality cannot be based on happiness; moral principles have to be derived from practical reason alone.

(Earlier published as an OpEd in *The Indian Express*, April 6, 2018)

55

Evaluating the Success of the Swachh Bharat Abhiyan

October 2, 2017, the birth anniversary of Mahatma Gandhi, also marked the third anniversary of the Modi's government's flagship scheme, the Swachh Bharat Abhiyan (SBA). The SBA is one of the largest cleanliness drives in the world, with a workforce of three million government employees who are directly or indirectly attached to the programme. With the SBA now completing three years, it is imperative to evaluate its achievements.

The Swachh Survekshan 2017 was undertaken by the Quality Council of India to check the progress and impact of SBA. The parameters of evaluation included waste collection (sweeping and transportation), municipal solid waste processing and disposal, open defecation and toilets, capacity building and information, and education and behaviour change. For a programme as diverse in impact as the SBA, these parameters will give us an idea of how it has been implemented but to think that they can tell us how the programme has done within a community is illogical.

Simple logic tells us that the single most important impact of the SBA should be on the health of the community. From the era of English physician John Snow, we know that cleanliness drives away diseases and promotes health, and therefore the success of such a programme should also be evaluated using some health parameters. The health of a community is undoubtedly influenced by a clean environment but multiple factors play a vital role in its acquisition and maintenance.

Hence, it is essential to use parameters that are objective and yet tell us the short-term outcomes of a cleanliness drive like the SBA.

One such parameter could be the reduction in the number of epidemics after the launch of the programme. Epidemics, particularly vector-borne epidemics (like malaria and dengue) and water-borne epidemics (like cholera and hepatitis) are considered by public health experts to be the most important determinant of cleanliness of the environment vis-à-vis its impact on the health of the community. Hence, an effective cleanliness drive should be impactful enough to reduce the number of epidemics reported from within the community.

The Integrated Disease Surveillance Programme run by the National Centre for Disease Control (under the Directorate General of Health Services) maintains an epidemic outbreak web portal that is regularly updated and, since 2009, any outbreak is reported on a weekly basis. An analysis of this data reveals some interesting facts. Selecting random years and random weeks, the data was divided into before and after October 2, 2014 (the launch date of the SBA), and was evaluated for epidemics that are directly related to cleanliness of the surroundings. Most epidemics fall in this category barring a few (like measles) and these were thus not considered in the final evaluation. An evaluation of the weeks 1, 16, 32 and 48 were done for 2011, 2012, 2013, 2015, 2016 and 2017 (2014 was not evaluated as it was the year of inception and week 48 in 2017 was also not evaluated); 2011-2013 were considered as "before" and 2015-2017 as the "after" groups. Statistical evaluation revealed that there is a difference in the mean number of alerts/outbreaks of 7.7 in week 1, 11 in week 16 and 0 in week 32 of the respective years between the two groups. The data shows that there is no decrease in incidence of outbreaks/alerts in the studied weeks in the "after" group. In fact, there is an increase in week 1 and week 16 in the "after group", which is not significant statistically.

This epidemic outbreak data raises important questions about the success of the SBA and the logic behind it. If the massive cleanliness drive has not been able to control epidemics on a short term, what long-term outcomes can we expect from it? Controlling epidemics like dengue, chikungunya and hepatits-E is directly related to cleanliness and hence any success with the SBA should have made some dent in the outbreak of these epidemics, but the current data shows otherwise.

The SBA's lack of success in reducing the number of epidemic outbreaks can be related to multiple factors like poor management of the programme on ground, inability to identify areas of thrust, and a poor prioritization of aims and targets within the programme itself. It appears that the main aim of the SBA is to reduce open defecation in the community, which is important. But had this too been achieved to a measurable degree, the outbreak of epidemics should have gone down.

The SBA is an ambitious project that aims to change people's perception of and behaviour towards cleanliness. The success of such programmes hinges on its ability to undergo scrutiny and constant audit so that the shortcomings can be addressed. By not using tangible and reproducible statistical parameters of health in the audit cycle of the programme, we are subjecting it to falsehood and therefore reducing its worth in bringing about any perceptible change. The SBA in its present form can be best viewed as a "toilet training" of the Indian masses with no significant contribution to their health, or so it appears from the data on epidemics. Reports from across the country have shown that toilets have been constructed as part of the programme but their use remains elusive for various logistical and social reasons. To improve the outreach and acceptability of the SBA it is necessary that people are clearly shown what good it can do to their health. It is unfortunate that in the very year in which the SBA was launched, the government slashed the health budget by around 20 per cent. It is essential to understand that swachta and health are complementary to each other and therefore a horizontal approach to link the two is vital.

(Earlier published in *The Wire*, November 13, 2017)

56

Healthcare Is a Serious State Responsibility and Should Be Kept Insulated From Populism

Of the important takeaways from the 2018 Union Budget, the proposal of launching a flagship National Health Protection Scheme (NHPS) has been hailed by many as one of the most important steps by the present government towards '*vikas*' or development. The proposed scheme plans to cover over ten crore poor and vulnerable families (which is approximately 50 crore beneficiaries,) providing coverage of up to Rs 5 lakh per family per year for secondary and tertiary care hospitalization.

We are told that this is the "world's largest government-funded healthcare programme"—although it must be clarified that it is not the world's largest expenditure on health, but only the largest number of people covered by a programme, that too when it becomes fully functional, which will not happen in the next six months at least (as told). If countries are run by intent (which in all honesty does matter to an extent) then there should be loud applause for the said scheme and its architects. The applause should be longer and louder, keeping in mind that the same government and the same Finance Minister in his very first Budget in 2014 had slashed health expenditure by around 20 per cent.

It took four years (and may be a few lakh deaths and countless sick) for the present regime to realize that budgetary allocation to health schemes is essential in a country like ours. But every applause should be followed by appraisal and evaluation. It is important to evaluate the details in the proposed scheme and see if the honourable Finance Minister's words in parliament are actually turned into reality, or end up as mere rhetoric.

To begin with, a government-funded health insurance scheme is not new in India. The Rashtriya Swasthya Bima Yojana (RSBY), which was launched in 2008, provided for an annual coverage of Rs. 30,000 to families living below the poverty line for treatment of diseases. The balance of the premium in the RSBY is subsidized and shared by the central (75 per cent) and the state (25 per cent) governments. The RSBY has an enrolment rate of more than 36 million families and the scheme has been hailed by the United Nations and the International Labour Organization, besides other international bodies.

Despite the proclaimed success of the RSBY, the scheme has been under ignominy for obvious loss of public money to private players. In an article in *The Lancet* in June 2016, it was shown that in RSBY, more than 80 per cent of the reimbursements went to the private sector. Besides, the scheme has also been under scrutiny of the comptroller and auditor general of India for all the wrong reasons.

Thus, government health insurance schemes do exist but with an obvious advantage to the private players in the game. The increase in allocation of money in the NHPS to Rs. 5 lakhs is a moment of "aha" for healthcare providers like us, but there is, and should be, a worry of further increase in the 'legitimate leak' of public money into the private sector. I am sure there is a definite (but difficult) method to prevent this leak by strengthening the public healthcare infrastructure, thereby making the scheme more comprehensive and robust. In the absence of this committed strengthening of public healthcare infrastructure, the "aha" moment of the hour will be reduced to an "alas" moment of despair.

Besides preventing private players to run amok in the garb of the new scheme, it is also essential that the government comes clear on the funding of the proposed NHPS. In his speech, the Finance Minister said, "Adequate funds will be provided for smooth implementation of this programme." What are these adequate funds? The Finance Minister has allocated a sum of Rs. 2,000 crores for the initial part of the scheme. Unfortunately, the mathematics involved in the realization of the NHPS makes it look surreal, a mere *jumla*.

For argument's sake, if we accept that when the scheme is fully functional, the same arithmetic which governs the RSBY remains valid, then the premiums shared by the central and state governments will be 75 per cent and 25 per cent, respectively. In RSBY, the enrolment in robust states like Tamil Nadu and Karnataka is around 57 per cent (which, by the way, is considered low by public health experts) of which around 10 per cent to 15 per cent avail of the scheme (this, too, is extremely variable depending on the people's confidence in the scheme and other socio-cultural factors).

Independently-available National Sample Survey healthcare utilization and expenditure survey data (2014) suggests that an average of 0.4 hospitalizations per person happen in the country.

Thus, the NHPS appears to be a utopian idea. To believe that it will change the landscape of India's healthcare utilization and reduce the impoverishment caused by diseases is not only far-fetched, but seriously flawed owing to the extreme paucity of money allocated to the same. What we need are small-scale, community-based health insurance programmes, as it has been shown throughout the world that such schemes raise healthcare utilization and lower the household financial burden. An even better idea would have been to actually increase the spending on health (read health infrastructure) and give some competition to countries like Bhutan and Ethiopia which spend significantly more than us on health. Healthcare is a serious state responsibility and responsibilities should be kept insulated from populism.

(Earlier published in *The Wire*, February 3, 2017)

57

Long Live India (Ayushman Bharat) in Times of Capitalism!

Thirty-year-old Aarti Devi (name changed) stared incredulously as I prescribed analgesics for her back pain. No, she wasn't unhappy with the treatment, but was troubled because I had prescribed analgesics three times a day after meals, on a full stomach. I realized that buying analgesics was not an issue. Getting three square meals a day, however, was.

In India, the ruptures within the healthcare delivery system do not pertain merely to issues of infrastructure or want of capital, they go far beyond. Thus, it is imperative to analyse the government's flagship programme—Ayushman Bharat—within the context of the unique combination of India's staggering poverty and vulgar capitalism.

In his interaction at the Express Idea Exchange, the CEO of Ayushman Bharat, Dr. Indu Bhushan, asked what was wrong with providing resources to the private sector to ensure services for the poor. He meant that besides public healthcare facilities, this was the first opportunity in the country's 71 years of sovereign existence that the poor will have access to private healthcare as well. There is significant optimism, if not inanity, in this assertion, because our brush with private players over a broad spectrum of involvements in the past has been far from pleasant.

From privatization of roads to water bodies, to the killer Blueline buses of Delhi, most private ventures of the government have resoundingly failed. How, then, can we assume that the private healthcare providers in the country will behave differently? It is an open secret that most private hospitals in Delhi fail to provide free treatment and beds to poor patients, despite this being a legal requirement in lieu of the land given at the time of their construction. If this can happen in the country's capital, we can only imagine the situation in smaller towns and cities.

The government is none the wiser following the lessons learnt from the Rashtriya Swasth Bima Yojna (RSBY), a programme not very different from Ayushman Bharat, started by the previous regime. It entitled poor families for treatment of up to Rs. 30,000 per year. In 2016, RSBY data revealed that 80 per cent of reimbursements under the scheme were made to private enterprises. It might not be wrong to label these reimbursements as a legitimate loot of public money.

Unfortunately, post neo-liberalization there have been persistent efforts to blur the boundaries between public and private funded healthcare, resulting in perilous repercussions in a developing country like ours. More than 80 per cent of healthcare in India is provided by private facilities. Poor medical regulation, ethical concerns, issues of class and caste differentiations and non-availability of adequate facilities in the hinterlands of the country, remain major obstacles to the adequate delivery of healthcare through such private players.

Patients like Aarti would never be able to seek treatment in a posh corporate hospital of Delhi, despite Ayushman Bharat. Too many socio-economic barriers will either restrict her entry or limit her persistence with treatment in one of these 'luxury' hospitals. Thus, opening private healthcare setups to insurance capitals without taking care of the said obstacles will have disastrous results.

A better, yet more tedious option would have been to iron-out the rules governing the interface between the two treatment sectors even before thinking of launching a scheme like Ayushman Bharat. An even better approach would have been to restructure the regulation of healthcare delivery so that more robust outcomes could be ensured through the scheme. Depending less on the insurance model within Ayushman Bharat would have been equally effective in providing a more comprehensive healthcare delivery system.

An equally intriguing aspect of the scheme is its inattention to the primary healthcare setup. The main focus, it seems, is on secondary and tertiary healthcare facilities. Having said this, the scheme plans to create 1,50,000 Health and Wellness Centres (HWC), which are essentially uplifted extant Sub Centres. Economic experts like Prabhat Patnaik, have carefully evaluated the scheme and shown that the money allocated in the 2018-19 union budget for the creation of these HWCs is merely Rs. 80,000 per centre.

This meagre allocation is not only insufficient for an effective upliftment, but also a blow to the very concept of Universal Health Care (UHC), as described by the World Health Organization (WHO). The essence of UHC appears to have been lost in the din of the scheme. For an effective UHC, the starting point should have been the PHCs—with an emphasis on prophylactic aspects of healthcare. The insurance model of the scheme is an incentive-based model which will promote the therapeutic aspect of healthcare in the country, leading to extra diagnostics and superfluous treatment strategies.

The complexities of healthcare delivery in India are many. With the pursuit of neoliberal policies, the divide between the 'haves' and the 'have-nots' is at an unprecedented level. We rank poorly in the world hunger index, the malnutrition index and on other parameters of health. What we needed were small-scale, community-based health insurance programmes, as it has been shown throughout the world that such schemes raise healthcare utilization and lower the household financial burden.

An even better idea would have been to increase the spending on health for the simple reason that it is the sole responsibility of the state. The political leadership of the country should realize that our experiments with insurance-based models of healthcare have failed in the past. According to Karl Marx, history repeats itself, first as tragedy, second as farce.

(Earlier published in *The Wire* under a different title, December 20, 2018)

58

The Cancer Refugees

Ramkishan Yadav (name changed) hails from Begusarai district in Bihar. He has been in Delhi for the past seven months to complete the treatment of his 11-year-old son, who suffers from a "treatable" form of bone cancer. The father and son live on the footpath in front of the main gate of the All India Institute of Medical Sciences (AIIMS) in the national capital. When they first arrived in the city, they had rented a room nearby. As the treatment got prolonged, they ran out of money. The room became a luxury and the family moved out into the street. The ordeal that Yadav and his son are going through, unfortunately, is not exceptional.

A visit to the road outside AIIMS late in the evening will indicate that hundreds of patients and bystanders have made it their home as they wait for their treatment to be over. A quick on-site survey reveals that many of these "temporarily homeless" people happen to be suffering from various forms of cancer. Cancer patients require long-term treatment and the public space outside the hospital offers quick access to the hospital services, more so in case of an emergency, which is not uncommon in this subset of patients. Such "cancer refugees" can be found on streets outside most big cancer centres of the country, in Delhi, Mumbai and so on.

In the absence of good peripheral cancer treatment centres, patients are referred to tertiary centres which are mainly located in big cities like Delhi, Mumbai, Chennai and Ahmedabad. Most of these patients have a typical history. They suffer from a curable form of cancer (hence the temptation to complete treatment) and are usually from distant places. The initial few months of treatment are "good" with a place rented for stay near the hospital. Once the money runs out, which usually happens in three to four months, the patients and their families are forced to shift to the streets next to the hospital.

Poverty caused by health expenditure has doubled in India in the past 15 years. A recent study claims that out-of-pocket health expenditure in India accounts for nearly 7 per cent of household expenses. Diseases like cancer are most damaging to a family's finances. In the absence of health and social security nets, cancers, particularly the ones that offer a chance of cure, can be financially debilitating for a family. It has been established the world over that poverty is a risk factor for cancer causation. But equally true is the fact that in countries like ours, cancer (treatment) is an important risk factor for tipping the balance, especially for families that live on the edge of absolute poverty. So not only does poverty cause cancer, cancer also causes poverty, at least in India. Cancer refugees represent the very phenomenon of "cancer poverty".

Over the last few decades, the incidence of cancer in India has increased. More than 1 million new cases of cancer are diagnosed every year and 6,00,000 to 7,00,000 cancer deaths were reported in the country in 2012-13. A study published in *Lancet Oncology* in May 2014 concluded that social factors, especially inequalities, are major determinants of India's cancer burden, with poorer people more likely to die from cancer before the age of 70 years than those who are more affluent.

The renowned Swiss medical historian, H.E. Sigerist once stated that "in any given society the incidence of illness is largely determined by economic factors" and "the problem of public health is ultimately political". Nothing can be closer to the truth. Cancer poverty calls for political solutions. The government must build more cancer care hospitals in the peripheral regions of the country and reduce the patient load of tertiary cancer centres. This requires rebooting priorities and giving emphasis to cancer as a public health issue.

Short-term solutions can be the development of basic shelters for cancer refugees at hospitals. Such shelters do exist, but they are far and few. For instance, in and around AIIMS Delhi, the government and public trusts run dharamshalas that offer over 400 beds. With a daily influx of more than 10,000 outpatients, these dharamshalas are always full and most patients have to either rent accommodation or live on the street. Patient shelters have to become a part of urban infrastructure.

A society that cannot take care of its sick is seriously ill.

(Earlier published as an OpEd in *The Indian Express*, July 23, 2018)

59

Diagnosing Bias

The Delhi High Court has ordered the formation of a committee of experts to examine if students with hearing impairment and dyslexia can pursue MBBS/BDS courses (Indian Express, August 10). This order came after two cases of students with the said disabilities were denied admission to medical colleges. The court's order has opened up a debate on two important aspects of the social attitude towards those with physical and mental disabilities: One, the actual inability of those who are physically challenged to perform a task. Two, whether those with specific physical and mental disabilities should be allowed to become doctors.

The inability of those who suffer from physical disabilities is now a matter of hollow words. We have ample examples from various fields (including medicine) where those with disabilities have excelled. From Stephen Hawking to Frida Kahlo to the Academy Award-winning actress Marlee Matlin, the spectrum of those with disabilities is not only just wide but also unique.

What impedes special people is not their disability but rather the inability of society to provide opportunities for accessibility, and acceptance. Even if we argue that the names mentioned above are an exception because of their individual brilliance, technological progress has opened new spheres of care, functionality and hence, inclusiveness. With the future of this technological tsunami not known, the inability of those with disabilities is nothing more than a figment of a non-inclusive thought process.

Having said that, in India, despite the efforts of successive governments and activists, disability continues to be a social taboo, a concrete wall which remains unscaled.

Not unexpectedly, doctors with disabilities are a minuscule part of any population. In a study in the United States, it was seen that more than 20 per cent of Americans live with a disability but only 2 per cent of practising physicians have disabilities. In the absence of scientific studies, this figure remains unknown in India. Despite the tiny numbers, most advanced countries have associations and societies of physicians with disabilities. They not only fight for the rights of their members but also conduct studies to evaluate the functionality and patient attitudes towards doctors with disabilities. Most of these associations work within the purview of the American Disability Act. In the presence of such a strong and effective statute, the associations are provided with teeth to look into issues with the medical curricula, which are disabled-friendly and ensure that they are adopted throughout the country. This is in striking contrast to the problem in our country where I am not aware of any such association or organization. Even the recently formulated Right of Persons with Disabilities Act, 2016, has not focused on the subject in detail.

Doctors, if not the first, are surely the most important contact point for the diseased and the disabled. Simply put, the skills of a physician are nothing more than the practice of compassion. A person with disabilities will be more understanding towards a patient in a similar situation. It is a feeble argument that those with disabilities cannot perform specific skills needed for the practice of medicine. The commonest plea I have heard is, "how can a doctor with congenital absence of an upper limb perform a Cardio Pulmonary Resuscitation (CPR)?" Surely he/she can't. But pathologists, microbiologists, anatomists, dermatologists and many others might have never performed a CPR.

Thus, there is a need to understand that disability is not the problem but rather it is our inability to modify our medical curricula to be more willing to include students with physical and mental disabilities. The need is to redefine the technical standards and counselling competencies of medical education institutes to better define the needs of medical students with disabilities. Exclusion is the mark of a regressive society.

(Earlier published as an OpEd in
The Indian Express, August 14, 2018)

60

Cure that Hurts

An important expose (Indian Express, August 25) has revealed that the Indian arm of Johnson and Johnson (J&J), a leading global pharma major, "suppressed" key facts on the harmful aftermath of surgeries conducted on hundreds of patients in the country using "faulty" hip replacement systems imported by the company. The report also revealed that J&J did not provide compensation to all the affected patients. An expert committee of the Union Ministry of Health and Family Welfare (MoHFW) had recommended that the pharma giant provide compensation to the patients who had undergone a surgery to implant the faulty device.

In fact, J&J did not even provide a list of all the 4,700 patients who had undergone the surgery to the concerned committee. This is a breach of medical ethics and moral principles and J&J stands exposed as a classical example of corporate high handedness, emboldened by administrative flaws and poor procedures of accountability.

It is important to unravel this violation of patients' rights because that will help us to be vigilant against future malpractices by international pharma firms. The J&J case makes for an interesting study of the factors that interact to "manufacture" a public health catastrophe.

First, there is a booming market for joint replacement in India. A recent survey projects that the joint replacement market will grow at an annual rate of around 25 per cent to 30 per cent over the next five to seven years. These are impressive figures and billions of dollars are at stake. It would be naive to believe that such a market would remain untouched by multinationals like J&J.

Joint replacement, like cardiac stenting, is a robust and useful technology. However, the need for a medical implant is governed not just by its utility and ease of use but also by the hype generated around it. An interesting study based, on the data of the Australian Orthopaedic Association National Joint Replacement Registry published in November 2017, revealed that a greater number of hip replacements happens in the more advantaged groups as compared to the disadvantaged population with a similar incidence of disease. This makes a physician's offer of hip replacement to a patient more arbitrary than has been considered so far.

It is important to remember that two important events accelerated the country's descent into a healthcare nightmare: The uncontrolled opening up of Indian markets in the 1990s and the country ratifying the World Trade Organization (WTO), which led to it becoming fully compliant with Trade Related Intellectual Property Rights (TRIPS) in January 2005. The latter made it easy for pharma companies to carry out clinical trials in the country. There was an influx of international companies who claimed to provide the state-of-the-art drugs, implants and technologies to doctors and patients, mostly in the garb of clinical trials. The absence of rigorous regulations led to serious violations of patients' rights, as was evident from the Human Papilloma Virus (HPV) Vaccine Clinical Trial Scam in 2009. It is believed that between 2005 and 2012, more than 2,000 patients have died across the country while participating in clinical trials conducted by pharma companies.

Second, it is critical to note that J&J in the US behaves much better than it does in India. The company has settled more than 9,000 lawsuits over the defective hip model in question for around $4.4 billion between 2013 and 2015. Since 2015, juries in the US have awarded $1.7 billion as compensation over the hip implants. So why does the pharma major behave as it does in India? Why has the company been high-handed and careless, as the MoHWF expert committee suggests? Much of this has to do with with the regulatory deficit in the medical devices market. The data suggests that technology assessment for medical devices and quality control methods in the country do not compare well with those in the Western world. Unfortunately, the National Medical Device Policy 2015 is still being debated in policy circles.

Finally, poor regulation of clinical practices is a reason for errant medical giants going unpunished. It is no secret that pharmaceutical companies and medical device manufacturers sponsor foreign trips, national and international conferences and even vacations of physicians. Doctors serve on the payrolls of medical device companies. They promote implants, including the faulty hip replacement device in question. It would thus be naïve to expect criticism of faulty implants or reporting of a serious side effect by surgeons or physicians obliged to the companies that manufacture them. Poor regulation of clinical practice not only emboldens pharma giants like J&J but also reduces the burden of their guilt. The poor medical ethics of the Indian physician serves their interests well.

The unethical behaviour of J&J is neither the first nor the last episode in the ongoing tragedy that is the saga of the poor Indian patient. With a poor regulatory mechanism, a corrupt healthcare system and a greedy doctor at their doorstep, such companies and their businesses stand to thrive in the graveyard of India's healthcare. The medical community must decide: Do we want to be part of the colossal injustice heaped on the patient, or call out suspected malpractices when we see them? After all, even the most comprehensive ethical system is of no use if the people it is meant for lack the will to do what is right.

(Earlier published as an OpEd in *The Indian Express*, August 30, 2018)

61

A Cure Called Inclusion

A report in *The Indian Express* ('Health to Poverty: Tribals Scrape Bottom of Barrel', Indian Express, September 15) drew our attention to the findings of an Expert Committee on Tribal Health appointed five years ago by the Ministries of Health and Family Welfare and Tribal Development. The report revealed that tribal communities lag behind the general population on most health parameters. This should not surprise us. Health is an under-discussed matter, both for the country's political class and a significant section of its civil society. Discussions on health-related problems of tribals, minorities and Dalits are even rarer, both in the corridors of power and within the educated social class of the country.

It is well-known that health is an interplay of a number of social, political, cultural, environmental and genetic factors. It is important, then, to identify the missing links in this sad story of tribal health in India. According to the 2011 Census, Scheduled Tribes form 8.6 per cent of the country's populations. Many of these tribes live in the most inaccessible geographical regions of the country. In fact, in a study, published in *The Lancet* in May, India ranked 145 among 195 countries in terms of healthcare accessibility—behind Bangladesh and Bhutan.

Access to healthcare depends on a number of factors of which female literacy is an important determinant—it is instrumental in shaping a group's healthcare seeking behaviour. According to the 2011 Census, the female literacy of Scheduled Tribes is 56.5 per cent; this is almost 10 per cent below the national rate and is one reason for tribal groups doing poorly on health parameters. Financial insecurity is another major cause of the ill-health of tribal people. It is no accident that a majority of hunger deaths reported in the country in the past five years happened to be of members of Scheduled Tribes.

The poor health of an ethnic group is very often a result of the exclusion of that group from a country's national imagination. Unfortunately, such exclusion is not unique to India. The infant mortality rate of native North Americans and Alaskan natives, both underprivileged groups in the US, is 60 per cent higher than that of the Caucasians. According to 2012 figures, more than 6 per cent people from these groups suffer from tuberculosis—compared to 0.8 per cent for the US's white population. A poll conducted by the Robert Wood Johnson Foundation and Harvard TH Chan School of Public Health revealed that about a quarter of Native Americans experienced discrimination when consulting a doctor or a health clinic. Aboriginal and Torres Strait Islander people in Australia are also known to have poorer health compared to other Australians. Exclusion and marginalization of a group leads to poverty, which in turn makes people from such groups vulnerable to diseases. This holds true for India's Scheduled Tribes as well. Ending the marginalization of tribal communities should then be at the heart of all government and civil society efforts to improve the health of people from tribal communities.

Universal healthcare is much more than providing infrastructure or alleviating specific health disorders through national programmes. It requires correction of a number of social parameters that govern health. Besides government apathy, problems specific to some tribal groups contribute to their poor health statistics. A 2004 study in Jhagram block of West Bengal's Medinipur district, for example, showed that 63.6 per cent Santhal (a Scheduled Tribe) mothers were aware of family planning measures, as compared to 87 per cent non-Santhal women. Moreover, some Scheduled Tribe communities are known to be vulnerable to specific diseases—people of Odisha's Gond tribe, for example, are susceptible to sickle cell disease.

Improving the health of Scheduled Tribes requires a multi-pronged approach. However, honest attempts at inclusion—politically, administratively and socially—should be behind all such endeavours. Measures to tackle group-specific health issues and capacity building of a group would go a long way in promoting their health.

(Earlier published as an OpEd in *The Indian Express*, August 30, 2018)

62
Implant Files: Who Should Own Upto What?

The recent exposé of the poorly regulated medical device industry by the International Consortium of Investigative Journalists (ICIJ) and *The Indian Express* highlights a matter of grave concern. The worldwide investigations revealed flaws in the medical device market in more than 36 countries. But in my opinion, the India revelations are the most serious and, unfortunately, the most worrisome because we have seen in the past that despite evidence against offenders, hardly any action is taken against them. A similar investigation, the Panama Papers by the ICIJ, did not result in any punitive action in our country (though cases are pending before courts of law) even when in Pakistan a court case sealed the fate of a sitting Prime Minister in the same scandal.

The exposé has not only thrown up some disturbing facts on medical devices and their poor regulation but has also exposed the intrinsic faultlines in the Indian healthcare system. The "Implant Files" show that from the implant manufacturer to the treating physician, impunity pervades the system. The findings make us understand that the interplay between the device manufacturer (or supplier), the end-user, namely the physician, and the regulator, namely the government, is not only complex but also full of opportunities for financial gain and hence wrongdoing is becoming the norm, not the exception.

The implant market in India should thus be seen in the context of the implant manufacturer, the physician and the government. Of the three arms of this unholy trio, the device manufacturer is the one who is exceptionally brazen as we have already seen in the Johnson & Johnson hip replacement case. What more should we expect from a multinational company? It should be clear to us that the implant manufacturers who bring their stuff to the Indian market do so only for one purpose—to earn money.

The implant industry in India is currently valued at $5.2 billion and contributes 4-5 per cent to the $96.7 billion Indian healthcare industry. This enormous amount is up for grabs and to believe that the implant manufacturers will not be using this opportunity to earn by all means, legal or otherwise, would be naive. In the process of implant promotion, the expose has shown how gimmicks like live surgeries are arranged by multinational implant companies. These "live surgeries" are performed by both national and international experts. In this regard, the stories of Rameshbhai Dodhiya, Dinesh Pillai and Raman Singh, as revealed in *The Indian Express*, are a chilling reminder of how these companies can behave if surgeries go wrong.

The culpability for this should be equally shared by the operating surgeon, the implant manufacturer and the local surgeon who organizes the live surgery. But in the absence of specific regulating guidelines, implant manufacturers continue to organize such live surgeries over gullible patients in the name of "professional education programmes and continuing medical education", as has been revealed by the Implant Files. Multinational implant giants should be made to realize that implant misuse is as grave an offence in India as it is in Western countries. The arrogance of the multinational implant companies in India needs to be urgently reined in.

The second weak link in the Implant Files is the treating physician. The exposé has shown that freebies are distributed among doctors by the implant and pharma companies to promote their products. Implant Files revealed that the cardiac stent manufacturer, Medtronic, gave away Rs. 50 crores worth of freebies as "product giveaways" to doctors over four years. Doctors becoming "brand ambassadors" for drugs and implants is an open secret in the Indian medical bazaar.

The poor reporting of adverse events for a drug or an implant by the treating physician is rampant in India. The expose showed that till 2014, adverse events were hardly reported by the Indian physicians or the manufacturer. Even after the formation of what is called the "Medical Device Adverse Event" (MDAE) report, the initial reporting of adverse events was minimal. Compared to this, the exposé revealed that in the UK regulators received 62,000 "adverse incident" reports linked to medical devices between 2015-18.

The inappropriate behaviour of the Indian physician has led to the erosion of trust among patients. No wonder the physician, considered to be God by a large chunk of Indian patients, is fast losing the halo. Unfortunately, the regulation of the Indian physician is also not a streamlined process. The confusion within the administration of the Medical Council of India (MCI), with multiple laws passed every other year for the governance of the apex body, has only added to the inappropriate behaviour of the Indian physician.

The MCI or any physician regulating body which replaces it in future needs to be robust in taking immediate punitive action against doctors involved in misappropriation of implants and drugs. It is worth mentioning that the General Medical Council (GMC), the physician regulating body in the United Kingdom, is a doctor administered body which has formulated strict laws for its own doctors. We need to learn from the GMC.

Finally, the onus of implant misappropriation lies with the government because it is the single agency which can regulate both the implant manufacturers and the physicians. A political will in this respect is essential. The exposé has shown that device companies in India are not regulated as per local standards but are dependent on the standards set by either the European regulators or the American FDA. This is a major loophole which is used by the implant manufacturers. The Implant Files reveal that successive governments in India have neglected the medical device sector.

The proposed Medical Device Regulation Bill is still to see the light of day. First drafted in 2006, it is interesting to note that in 2016 it was decided that the bill be converted and introduced only as medical device rules and regulations, applicable from 2018. The Implant Files revealed that this delay in bringing a law and converting it into an executive order was because the bureaucracy of the day felt that a separate bill will bring in "more control" and "curtail growth and innovation" in the medical device industry.

We can very well imagine that if there is reluctance in the highest offices of the executive, it will be nearly impossible to regulate this ever expanding market of implants in the country. In fact, the Implant Files reveal that under the new rule, despite an estimated 5,000 medical devices being sold in the country, the categories of medical devices "notified" and, therefore regulated, number only 23. This is a serious flaw in a market which is supposedly the fourth-largest in Asia after Japan, China and South Korea. The regulations in these three countries are not only robust but also more people-friendly.

The Implant Files thus reveal a serious illness within the Indian medical implant and device market. This market is expected to grow to $50 billion by 2025. The onus of regulation of this ever growing market solely rests on the government of the day. For my fellow physicians, I am reminded of what Friedrich Nietzsche had once said, "I am not upset that you lied to me, I am upset that from now on I can't believe you."

(Earlier published as an OpEd in *The Indian Express*, December 22, 2018)

63

What Should Actually Make the Doctors Angry

The recent strike of doctors across Maharashtra (and other parts of the country) against violence unleashed on them by disgruntled relatives of patients have thrown up uncomfortable questions. Whenever and wherever, violence must be abhorred and condemned in all its forms. Undoubtedly, all healthcare providers should be ensured safety at places of work. Violence at workplaces can have negative and disastrous effects on the employee satisfaction and work performance. Having said this, it is also essential that the medical community should do an introspection and try and find the flaws within; flaws which need to be rectified to avoid ugly situations at work. Unfortunately, the medical fraternity either fails or turns a blind eye to realize that we live in a society which institutionalizes violence. The recent misbehaviour and violence (with impunity) by a Member of Parliament with an Air India employee is a glaring example of this. The real problem is when violence ceases to be violence, when it loses the contempt it deserves and this is what the young Indian doctors should be more concerned and angry about.

Violence as a means of justice is a common parlance in the present-day Indian society but a large part of the intellectual class (including doctors) remains insensitive to it till it turns on them. Working with some of the best brains in medicine in the country, I wonder how many of my seniors, colleagues and juniors would even know about the tombstones in India's graveyard of monumental injustices and violence. Unfortunately, most of my professional brethren have not even heard about the Khairlanji massacre, don't understand the reasons behind the Bhagalpur blindings, don't care about what happened at Naroda Patiya and fail to understand the logic behind the Narmada Bacahao Andolan. We, the doctors, live in a glass house where we see the society pass by but cannot feel its pain or share its grief. This insulated existence of the present-day doctor is in sharp contrast to the physicians of the years gone by. The family physicians of the 1960s and 70s were a part of the society they served, sharing each loss and every triumph.

In India, doctors are considered god, another fact which wraps each one of us with pride and to an extent arrogance. Having worked in the West, I have not seen this form of idolization of the medical practitioner where the doctor-patient relationship is nothing more than professional. We Indians have a penchant of accepting the divine status too soon. The acceptance of this god-like status by the Indian physician is also a cause of concern and a reason for violence against doctors. Gods are not supposed to mint money. Gods are not supposed to have flaws and if they do, the illiterate and the deprived faithful unleash violence to break the moulds they have so devotedly constructed. The doctors of the land should realize that acceptance of a divine status is the acceptance of violence as an adjunct unless they are prepared to sacrifice much more. The rampant corporatization of medical practice and erosion of medical ethics in private and public set ups is another reason why these 'gods' face the music now and then. Misbehaviour, over-treatment, under-treatment and blatantly expensive treatment forms an important part of the present-day medical culture but unfortunately not many among us are willing to fight against it. I am yet to find a statement by an authorized/statuary body of medicine or surgery in the country outrightly condemning malpractices of its own members. The Indian Medical Association, the Indian Orthopaedic Association and the Association of Surgeons of India maintain a pathetic silence in such matters. This hood winking continues till coercion from the other side becomes threatening.

Also, the medical fraternity and young doctors of our country should realize that we work with limitations of infrastructure. The poor conditions of government hospitals particularly in the interiors of the country is no secret. Lack of proper infrastructure leads to improper care and hence a threat of violence. With one doctor for every 2000 people, the situation is bound to get out of hand at times. Unjustified violence can be common practice. The working hours for residents who form the backbone of public funded healthcare is dreadfully out of proportion but no one, not even the medical fraternity, wants to raise the issue with the relevant administrative authorities. Thus, it would be prudent not to make any struggle as the present one in Maharashtra, a fight against the patients. It just cannot be doctors versus patients. Doctors cannot and should not turn against patients, in fact the anger should be used against the administrative lapses of infrastructure which lead to ugly scenes in hospitals. Efforts should be made on the part of the doctors to send the message that they are not against patients. A simple way to assert the point would have been to run out-patient clinics outside their hospitals during the days of strike.

Solutions like beefing up security within hospital premises can only provide temporary relief. Most solutions to the problem lie within the training of medical personnel. Sensitizing the budding doctor to the poor and the underprivileged can be a simple solution which would reap huge dividends in the long run. Compassion, unfortunately cannot be taught. Teaching behavioural sciences at undergraduate and post graduate levels can be helpful. Acquainting the young doctor to prejudices of the society is a method to make them stand against institutionalized violence which in turn will bring compassion. Thus, the young doctors should realize that the violence they suffer breeds within the society they live. To be insensitive to violence with others, is inviting violence to self.

(Earlier published at the *Countercurrents.org*, April 6, 2017)

64

Missing in the Polls

As about 900 million voters prepare to elect their next government, the agenda for the Indian elections is supposedly decided. But there is an eerie silence on the part of the political class and the general public around issues of health. In most elections in Western countries, the healthcare policies of a political party are an important agenda. During the May 2015 general elections in the UK, the prestigious medical journal, *The Lancet*, called the UK's National Health Services (NHS) a "political hot potato" for parties in that country. Unfortunately, in India, despite a dismal healthcare set up, health still does not figure in the imagination of the rulers or the ruled.

Six days after the terrorist attack in Pulwama, the World Health Organization (WHO) released its report on the global health expenditure, that not only reveals ground realities on health economics but also helps governments to prioritize future health expenditure. The report revealed that the global spending on health increased in low and middle-income countries by 6 per cent and in high-income countries by 4 per cent. It showed that both India and Pakistan have populations which are one of the highest in the world when it comes to spending out-of-pocket on health. However, its stark findings got lost in the din of a near-war between the two countries. The current infant mortality rate (IMR) in India stands at 44 per 1,000 live births and the country stood twelfth on a UNICEF list of 52 low-middle income countries with the highest IMR in the world (2016). India's neonatal mortality rate (NMR), at 25.4 per 1,000 live births, was higher than that of Sri Lanka, Bhutan, Nepal and Bangladesh. Only Pakistan and Afghanistan fared worse than us in the subcontinent.

Considered to be a sensitive indicator of the quality of healthcare delivery, the maternal mortality rate (MMR) for India is 130 per 1,00,000 live births. The average global MMR hovers around 216 per 1,00,000 live births. What is startling is the fact that the so-called electorally most sensitive state of the country, Uttar Pradesh, has an MMR of 201 per 1,00,000 live births. UP also happens to be the electoral state of the PM.

It is interesting to note that the word "health" or "healthcare" appeared 83 times in the election manifesto of the BJP and 42 times in the manifesto of the Congress Party during the run-up to the 2014 elections. Despite this, health did not become an election agenda. Even today, the Opposition does not want to make the Gorakhpur hospital children's deaths (from 2017) a pivotal point for their campaigns.

It is important to analyse why something as important as the health of a nation remains undiscussed during elections here. Illiteracy, lack of awareness, diversionary communal-caste discussions by the political class, lack of political will, and, poor electoral ethics are some of the reasons which come to mind. It would, perhaps, be preposterous to believe that the people would seek health from their rulers when basic survival issues like hunger, unemployment and education go unaccounted. Even as the country with the highest number of malnourished children in the world, our expectation for good healthcare seems like a pipe dream.

In view of the WHO report, however, the least we can expect from our political class is a general consensus on increasing public health funding. At present, we spend just around 1 per cent of the GDP on health. This is less than what even countries like Ethiopia and Bhutan spend on the health of their people. Most experts believe that we should be spending, at least, 3 per cent of the GDP on health. For achieving universal health coverage, it is imperative that domestic spending on health be increased. It is known that a health system with high government funding provides accessible and more affordable healthcare to its people, also ensuring financial protection of its citizens.The Swiss medical historian, H.E. Sigerist once said that "the problem of public health is ultimately political". As a mature democracy, there is an urgent need to make state-sponsored healthcare a crucial component of political campaigns during elections. As citizens of the largest democracy of the world, it is our duty to accept an electoral agenda that is as per our needs, not as per the wishes of politicians for whom hubris, rhetoric and hollow promises are routine.

(Earlier published as an OpEd in *The Indian Express*, March 26, 2019)

The Final Essay: The Summer I Want to Live

Will the swallows fly home this summer? Will the nightingale sing the ballad of hope ever again? And the tiny canary, caged into oblivion, will it fly back to where it belongs? Will this summer be like summer? I don't know.

But I know that the lifeless horizon is never forever. The dark night has to yield, however dark and however cold it may be. The rays of light are ushered into the darkness, thrust upon the soul of the night to turn it red. Red? Yes, red with the blood of hope and then yellow with warmth. Somehow, the ancient winter of Quasimodo has to give rise to the summer of Blake. The somehow, I don't know. The somehow which only hope can decipher.

And the swallows? What predicts their return? The smell of summer maybe. Or the warmth of the yellow horizon. I don't know but they still return. Somehow. They return flying over blue oceans, over valleys of flowers and over ruined cities. They fly, because to fly is to reach the zenith of truth. They return because to return is in them. Their stoic souls have tiny wings which flap at the yield of summer in the faraway lands. A summer where the orchards of hope will bloom and the mulberry tree will never lose its leaves to the chilly draughts of hate. The summer, I want to live.

But there are many who will not see this summer? Yes, I know their names. The gusty zephyrs have blown them away into a land which has no summers, no winters, no rains, no hate—the nothing land. The nothing land of immensity. How can we march into the summer without their memories tugged under the warmth of our beating hearts? They are/were the harbingers of this summer. They are that light of dawn which turns the night into day. Will not the returning swallows look for them? What if the yellow bubbly canary seeks for that little girl with the purple dress, who went missing looking for her ponies in the green meadows of hate? Will not the melodious koel ask for the way to the homes of those who left us? And the mulberry tree? Won't it refuse to bloom in their absence? And what will we say to the soft summer clouds who will wander on the blue sky looking for that brave person whose body was riddled with disgust? Won't they refuse to pour on this land to raise the wonderful smell of the wet summer earth? Yes, they fortunately will.

We will lie to them all. We can't risk the swallows not to return. We can't risk the koels not to sing again. The cruel, silent winters have frozen away few but that does not mean that the summers have to wait. And this summer, as precious as a child's new toy, has to come.

It has to come.

It has to come for the swallows and the koels. It has to come to thaw us from our stony ice coffins of hate. It has to come because the winters we faced have drawn out every morsel of life from our green trees and the singing birds. Not the gods of earth (or the gods of heaven) can halt this summer from emerging on us. This is a summer etched in stone over the graves of the martyrs who fought for its being. The long weeds of neglect which surround these graves have to be singed by the summer sun.

So does the approaching summer belong to the swallows, the canaries and the koels? I don't know. It probably belongs to all of them and to all of us and to those who sleep hungry under the shade of the mulberry tree. Summers, unlike the winters we passed through, cannot belong to the one who is all powerful with a large chest full of hate. We all have an entitlement to this summer. The swallows have to return home this summer.

This is the summer I want to live.